Is the East Still Red?

Socialism and the Market in China

Is the East Still Red?

Socialism and the Market in China

Gary Blank

zero
books

Winchester, UK
Washington, USA

First published by Zero Books, 2015
Zero Books is an imprint of John Hunt Publishing Ltd., Laurel House, Station Approach,
Alresford, Hants, SO24 9JH, UK
office1@jhpbooks.net
www.johnhuntpublishing.com
www.zero-books.net

For distributor details and how to order please visit the 'Ordering' section on our website.

Text copyright: Gary Blank 2014

ISBN: 978 1 78099 757 5

A CIP catalogue record for this book is available from the British Library.

Design: Stuart Davies

Printed in the USA by Edwards Brothers Malloy

We operate a distinctive and ethical publishing philosophy in all
areas of our business, from our global network of authors to
production and worldwide distribution.

CONTENTS

Dedicated to Janina Rowbicki—"Babcia"

Acknowledgements

In researching, writing, and revising this book, I gained sustenance and encouragement from many quarters. The first to be thanked are members of my family, especially my parents Rick Blank and Sandra Gryziak, who have always provided unflagging support and enthusiasm for my academic and political activities even when they weren't convinced of all the particulars. My sister, Kelly, offered encouraging words and infectious optimism when my own spirits flagged; and my brother, Sean, graciously agreed to read an earlier draft of the text at a particularly frenetic moment. My grandmother, Janina, generously opened up her home during summer months, providing unrivalled hospitality and companionship which more than offset the lonely solitude of research and writing. I am deeply grateful to them all for their love and support.

The primary concern of this book is the political economy of "state socialism" and capitalist market reform, and I was fortunate to be associated with two rather different communities who also shared this concern. The first are those I've known on the far left in Canada and the UK, mostly Trotskyists, who rightly argue that China has not simply "restored" capitalism but wrongly insist that the country is some form of "workers' state." Although I eventually rejected this dogma, I benefited greatly from the inquisitive, informed, and serious way in which these comrades engaged with the question. Many of them may not be persuaded by my arguments, but they should recognize a shared set of political and intellectual concerns.

The second community are students and faculty at the Department of Political Science at York University in Toronto, where I conducted the bulk of the work for this book while studying as a graduate student. The Department is one of the most vibrant, exciting and challenging places of its kind, with generous faculty members who do not shy away from demanding innovative, high quality work. Three deserve special recognition and thanks here: George Comninel, who introduced me to the historical materialist perspective that is so central to this book; and Hannes Lacher and Greg Albo, who supervised my early writing on the subject with immense patience, interest, and intellectual guidance. Of course, final responsibility for any factual errors and particularities of interpretation rest with me alone.

Finally, I owe special thanks and gratitude to my partner Christine Whyte. She consistently provided enthusiasm, inspiration and assistance throughout the project, even as my plaintive promises of needing "just one more day/afternoon/hour" to finish wore increasingly thin.

Chapter One

Introduction: Whither Chinese Socialism?

"If the twentieth century was dominated, more than by any other single event, by the trajectory of the Russian Revolution, the twenty-first will be shaped by the outcome of the Chinese Revolution."
—Perry Anderson[1]

"The Revolution is dead. Long live the Revolution!"
—Minqi Li[2]

With the sputtering and eventual collapse of "actually existing socialism" in the Soviet Union and Eastern Europe, an intense debate emerged within the left regarding the viability of alternatives to capitalism. For those who maintained that the failures of "state socialism" stemmed from centralized planning rather than collective ownership of the means of production, Chinese reforms in the early 1990s seemed to offer the prospect of a third way: "market socialism."[3] These progressive proponents of the market were answered by a number of more orthodox Marxist critics, who reasserted the traditional claim that markets and socialism are antithetical and that Beijing's dalliance with capital would simply lead to greater social violence and exploitation. Far from offering any desirable alternative to capitalism and neoliberal globalization, the Chinese path was simply "another road to barbarism."[4] The debate began to wane at the turn of the century, however, as ever fewer observers could detect any trace of socialism in a country that was instituting massive privatization of state industry and acceding to hundreds of "free market" conditionalities in order to join the World Trade Organization (WTO).

1

In recent years, though, it has become apparent that China's status as a non-capitalist, if not a *socialist*, alternative to prevailing developmental models is not yet a settled question among activists and critical political economists. Two works in particular have revived the debate: Martin Hart-Landsberg and Paul Burkett's *China and Socialism: Market Reforms and Class Struggle* (2004), and Giovanni Arrighi's *Adam Smith in Beijing: Lineages of the Twenty-First Century* (2007).[5] These two texts offer important analytical and empirical contributions in their own right and reflect broader left-wing debates on the future and efficacy of "socialism with Chinese characteristics." They have also served as intellectual lodestones for independent contributions and entire symposia in leading journals of critical analysis.[6] Reiterating traditional Marxist claims, Hart-Landsberg and Burkett maintain that Chinese market socialism was never more than an unstable and contradictory half-way house, paving the way to "full-fledged capitalist restoration, including growing foreign economic domination."[7] Arrighi offers a striking counter-claim: not only is the recent Chinese economic ascent a product of "non-capitalist market-based development,"[8] it also has the potential to dethrone Washington from its global hegemonic position, ushering in a "commonwealth of civilizations truly respectful of cultural differences."[9]

This book assesses China's status and potential as a *non-capitalist* developmental model through a close and critical examination of *China and Socialism* and *Adam Smith in Beijing*, informed by the authors' wider body of work, the contributions that have emerged in response, and some of the more pertinent empirical work generated by Sinologists and Asianists. It maintains that both analyses bring us only part of the way to a sufficient and comprehensive understanding of the contemporary political economy of the People's Republic of China (PRC). The *analytical* contradiction between the two works reflects *real* contradictions that have characterized the market reform process. Taken separately, each work only illuminates one side of this process; but considered together they begin to form the basis for an alternative historical materialist reading of the market socialist experience.

This is not to suggest that both contributions are of equal coherence and validity. Hart-Landsberg and Burkett's unapologetic Marxism provides a persuasive analytical framework for understanding the contradictory dynamics of market socialism, the intensifying exploitation and alienation of Chinese workers, and the dire need for a much deeper alternative than the Chinese Communist Party (CCP) leaders in Beijing have ever envisaged. For these reasons much of the Left has embraced their work as conclusive. *Adam Smith in Beijing*, while often admirable in scope and ambition, is too theoretically eclectic, empirically selective, and politically wishful to stand on its own as a definitive contribution, even among those who share Arrighi's sympathies.[10] This is reflective not just of Arrighi's particular approach, but also the more general difficulties of formulating a coherent theoretical basis for a political project that seeks to harmonize market competition with the traditional objectives and aims of socialism.[11] But the value of Arrighi's contribution lies not in the broad sweep of his analysis but rather in his agenda of concern. In asking fundamental questions about what makes a market specifically *capitalist*, drawing attention to the historical pedigree of non-capitalist market societies, and pointing to the enduring significance of "accumulation without dispossession" in contemporary China, Arrighi has drawn attention to theoretical and empirical issues that tend to be neglected in Marxist treatments, which generally rely on abstract models of capital accumulation. Thus, while Arrighi hardly upends the Marxist critique of Chinese market socialism, he does invite a reconsideration of its assumptions, a sharpening of its theoretical approach, and a widening of its empirical ambit.

China's political economy cannot be understood without the

conventional Marxist categories of primitive accumulation, class exploitation, and surplus extraction; but neither can it be comprehended without serious attention to its non-capitalist social forms, especially state industry and collectivized land. The central contention of this book is that the Chinese developmental experience of the past 20 years exhibits many of the central hallmarks of a transition toward capitalism. In this respect, a stable and durable market socialism, or "non-capitalist market society," is truly illusory. Yet this transition is not complete and is subject to serious contention by workers, peasants, and sections of the ruling stratum (CCP officials and enterprise managers) that reproduce themselves in non-capitalist ways. It is in this sense that China remains a "transitional" society whose future class character is not yet determined. Tracing this *process* of change is essential for understanding and intervening in contemporary social and political struggles.

The theoretical and empirical basis for a renewed historical materialist understanding of the Chinese alternative is established in several steps. The book begins by situating the work of Arrighi and Hart-Landsberg/Burkett within the broader intellectual and ideological trends that have influenced left-wing and critical analyses of China in the post-Mao and post-Soviet period. Contradictions and unanswered questions in both *China and Socialism* and *Adam Smith in Beijing* are exposed, shaping an analytical agenda for the discussion that follows. In different ways and for different reasons, both works fail to offer a sufficiently clear understanding of crucial concepts: the specificity of capitalism, the nature of socialism, and the political and social character of the 1949 Chinese Revolution. A few writers have suggested that a thorough reassessment of the "socialist transition" debate and the period of Maoist centralized planning are needed to comprehend the market reforms that followed.[12] I agree, but also suggest that coming to terms with the socialist transition debate requires an adequate understanding of the specificity of capitalism, which can only be acquired by engaging with the other "transition" debate concerning how European feudalism was transformed into capitalism.

The latter debate highlights the need to conceptualize capitalism as a unique system in which both producers and appropriators *depend* on the market for their reproduction. A number of pertinent theoretical insights follow from this: the peculiar separation of politics and economics in capitalist states, the global expansion of capitalism via processes of combined and uneven development, and the dynamics of bureaucratic collectivism. Making use of these categories, I argue that well into the 1990s, despite years of market reforms, China maintained a bureaucratic-collectivist system in which direct producers and bureaucrats were merged with the means of production, and politics and economics were fused. The incompatibility of planning and market efficiency compelled the CCP to push a counter-revolution from above: dispossessing workers, privatizing enterprises, subjecting officials to market-based performance evaluation, and generally effecting a separation of economics from politics (or a depoliticization of the economic sphere). However, the strategy was only partially successful. Class struggles, the imperatives of party-state legitimacy and power, and the reproductive strategies of individual officials and managers have all acted to frustrate capitalist restructuring. I illustrate this point by addressing several concrete themes: social relations in agriculture; reforms in industry; the dynamics of class struggle; intra-bureaucratic and intellectual dissent; the response of the Chinese state to the world economic crisis; and the concern among global and Chinese elites to correct global economic "imbalances."

Having engaged in a wide-ranging theoretical and empirical assessment of the Chinese alternative, I conclude by maintaining the People's Republic is indeed a "world-historical *novum*."[13] Having rejected the neo-liberal "shock therapy" prescriptions mandated for post-Soviet Russia, market socialist Beijing has ironically established much more hospitable conditions for dynamic capitalist development than "sale of the century" Moscow.[14] But by avoiding an outright repudiation of state property and socialist ideals, the bureaucrats in Beijing have not been able to fully extirpate non-capitalist ways of reproduction— nor is it clear that they can, at least if they wish to maintain the CCP's political monopoly. As a consequence, the Chinese leadership's aspiration for achieving a form of East Asian developmental state has been decisively blocked. The manner in which China's accumulating political economic contradictions are resolved—through either a "full-fledged capitalist restoration" or a reinvigoration of collectivized property forms and economic planning—will determine the Chinese Revolution's ultimate legacy for workers and peasants in China and the world. An important theme of this book is that strategies of "rightful resistance" have been effective in upsetting processes of primitive accumulation, but also that establishing a genuine socialist alternative will require the conquest of what has always been denied to Chinese toilers: a regime of workers' democracy.

Chapter Two

Leftist Assessments of Socialist China: Then and Now

The author of a 2006 UBS bank report on China aptly noted that "describing China's economy can resemble the tale of the blind men and the elephant; there's plenty of evidence to support the most contradictory arguments."[1] There are inherent difficulties in succinctly describing any political economy, of course, but they are especially acute for a country of China's history, size and complexity. What is held to be characteristic of one district, region, or province may not apply to another, just as what was deemed to be true in 1998 cannot be confidently maintained today. Even as there has been a profusion of case studies in Chinese political economy, an understanding of its totality has lagged far behind.

The fault lines dividing left analyses of Chinese political economy are not simply empirical but also conceptual and ideological. This is not to say that differences over empirical data are unimportant—they can be crucial, as will be shown, for example, with Hart-Landsberg and Burkett's understanding of property relations in the countryside. But ultimately more decisive is how empirical detail is integrated into a broader understanding of the social totality, and what concepts are employed to achieve this integration. What may seem to be relatively straightforward disagreements over empirical questions (such as the extent of privatization, marketization, and class polarization in the Chinese countryside) can mask more fundamental conceptual differences over how to interpret and prioritize the empirical data itself. In the Chinese case, the basic categories of "socialism" and "capitalism," as well as "plan" and "market," are frequently used to historically and analytically distinguish Maoist from post-Maoist China. Disagreements within the left over the character of China's political economy often reveal more about the presuppositions of their authors than they do about the reform process itself. The objective of this first section is to offer a brief survey of the shifting terrain in critical China studies, identifying the ways in which *China and Socialism* and *Adam Smith in Beijing* address previous deficiencies in the literature while instantiating others. After pointing out a number of pertinent questions left unanswered by both works, it is argued that a more rigorous interrogation of key concepts—not least capitalism and socialism—is required to advance beyond the impasse.

The antinomies of academic Maoism

Post-Soviet capitalist triumphalism weighed heavily on leftist imagination in the 1990s, and the field of China studies was certainly not spared. Elizabeth Perry, an eminent historian of Chinese working class struggles, recently noted that many Asianists of the 1968 generation were initially drawn to the field by a favourable view of the Chinese Revolution:

> The many budding young Asianists who soon joined the CCAS [Committee of Concerned Asian Scholars], myself included, were generally united in the conviction that the war in Vietnam represented an epochal clash between a dynamic Asian revolutionary upsurge, stirred by the example of Mao's China, on the one hand, and a destructive American imperialism, bolstered by the work of some prominent members of the Asian studies department, on the other.[2]

With such a romantic view of Maoist China's revolutionary potential, it is not surprising that starry eyes turned jaundiced. Bitter disappointment and dashed illusions provided a common substrate for the emergence of two, seemingly opposite, tendencies: on the one hand, repudiation of Maoist China in light of Deng's reforms; and on the other hand, fierce denunciation of the latter against an idealized construct of the former. Mark Selden and Edward Friedman are two prominent exemplars of the first reflex. In his classic work *The Yenan Way in Revolutionary China* (1971), Selden proclaimed: "The Chinese revolution offers inspiration not only to those who would expel colonial oppressors... It addresses men and women everywhere who seek to create a society free from stifling oppression, arbitrary state power, and enslaving technology."[3] Writing at a later date, Friedman was even more glowing: "Mao by the example of his struggle communicates the vigour of hope, the vitality of possibility, the vision of justice. Mao's message to the 20th century is elegantly simple: what should be can be."[4] By 2005, however, Selden, Friedman and their collaborator Paul Pickowitz were offering a remarkably different assessment in a co-authored work, suggesting that Mao's revolution had actually produced an oppressive and authoritarian state. "The more revolution advanced," claimed the authors, "the more... the state seemed parasitic... Revolutionary dynamics splintered society from the state, 'us' from 'them.'"[5] Friedman, for one, has become a breathless enthusiast of the current "China model," touting the alleged potential that Chinese export zones hold for "transform[ing] Africa."[6]

One of the most ardent critics of Selden and Friedman's turn was the late William Hinton—witness to the Chinese Revolution, celebrated author of *Fanshen*, and frequent contributor to the pro-Mao socialist periodical *Monthly Review*.[7] In the early 1990s, writers associated with that journal began to promote the "restoration" thesis, essentially a mirror opposite of the view advanced by Selden *et al* in which an unblemished version of Mao Zedong's "socialism" was contrasted with Deng Xiaoping's "capitalism."[8] In 1991, when Deng's economic reforms were still in a stage of comparative infancy, Hinton maintained that China had long been on the "capitalist road":

> China's Thermidor occurred in late 1978 when the Third Plenary Session of the Eleventh Central Committee, dominated by Deng Xiaoping and other survivors of the Liu Shaoqi clique, switched policies and began the "reform." This marked a shift from working-class power to bourgeois power, from working-class politics to bourgeois politics, from the socialist road to the capitalist road. At the meeting China changed colour, and from that time on new leaders began dismantling both the socialist economic base and the socialist superstructure that the Chinese people had built with such effort over thirty years.[9]

Minqi Li has echoed this analysis in recent years, lamenting that the "urban working class became politically passive and was caught off guard by the 1976 counter-revolutionary coup."[10] It is indeed an abrupt transformation, and it should raise some pointed questions. How could the People's Republic plummet from being a bastion of revolutionary socialism and working-class power with a single plenary session meeting? If the reform measures really did mark a shift "from working-class power to bourgeois power," why did they not arouse mass working-class opposition? *Monthly Review* writers have been unable to provide a satisfactory answer to these uncomfortable questions because they proceed from flawed assumptions. In truth, there was very little "working-class power" in Mao's day, a fact that calls into question Hinton's laudatory references to a "socialist economic base" and "socialist superstructure."

Between the antinomies provided by Selden/Friedman and Hinton/*Monthly Review* are a range of left views. These are not so much expressions of disappointment in the Maoist experiment as they are signs of resignation that such an experiment was doomed to fail, leading to frank, albeit grudging, resolutions that some variant of capitalism is the best that can be hoped for at present. Expressing sympathy for the ideals of Maoism, writers like Maurice Meisner and Victor Lippit have repeated the Deng regime's own proclamation that the productive forces in China were simply too weak to support rapid socialist construction, and that an extended period of capitalist development will be required before such ambitions can again be entertained. As the Mao era recedes ever more into the past, their assessments have gradually grown harsher. In his biography of Mao, Meisner concludes that "[w]hat material progress there was in the late Mao period hardly compensates for, indeed pales into insignificance, when weighed against the famine that issued from the Great Leap and the human and social destructiveness of the Cultural Revolution." The errors of late Maoism, in turn, stem from having "implicitly rejected many of the basic premises of Marxist theory. It was an ideology that ignored the Marxist insistence that capitalism was a progressive stage of development in world history and the necessary precondition for socialism."[11] For his part, Lippit once penned analyses of the "dynamics of socialist transition" in China, but now seems to have concluded that it was all for nought.[12] "The actual contest in China," he discovers, "was not between capitalism and socialism but between capitalism and statism…. Capitalism will have to play out its historic role before being supplanted."[13]

China and Socialism: An elaborated 'restoration' thesis

Hart-Landsberg and Burkett make clear that their harsh critique of China's political economy is intended as an intervention in current left debates—against those who would suggest that "China remains in some sense a socialist country," as well as those who "conclude that China is a development model, with a growth strategy that can and should be emulated by other countries."[14] The authors' normative commitment to a "working-class perspective"[15] is refreshing and commendable, and their explicitly Marxist orientation is a necessary and potentially powerful tool for analysing China's turn to the market. They outline an orthodox Marxist understanding of the capital-labor relation as necessarily exploitative, oppressive, and alienating; and they employ traditional historical materialist categories of analysis, like forces of production, relations of production, and the reserve army of labor. Most importantly, they highlight the "basic Marxist observation" that "capitalist development involves the social separation of workers from the necessary conditions of production, including natural conditions, and the conversion of these conditions and workers' labor power into means of producing commodities for a profit."[16]

However, while Hart-Landsberg and Burkett criticize other leftists for a lack of theoretical clarity, they often fail to provide such clarity themselves.[17] What is lacking is any sustained theoretical discussion of the distinguishing characteristics of socialism and the non-capitalist "transitional" or bureaucratically collectivized societies. Their perfunctory definition of socialism as "a system centered on grass-roots worker-community needs and capabilities"[18] is unobjectionable, but receives only two pages of elaboration at the end of their work. Without a clear specification of why and in what ways the Maoist planned economy was distinct from authentic socialism, the theoretical confusion that has long attended notions of socialism among critical China analysts is perpetuated, not dispelled.

This is unfortunate, for despite Hart-Landsberg and Burkett's intimations to the contrary, the notion that there has been a capitalist restoration in China is hardly alien to critical political economists. In fact, as Arrighi notes, during recent years it has become the "predominant view" among Western leftists,[19] in no small part because of the influence of *Monthly Review*. Indeed, most of the critiques of Arrighi's work that have appeared in prominent left journals display a general acceptance of the restoration thesis.[20] Still, *China and Socialism* improves upon the typical analyses of *Monthly Review* in at least two respects. First, it acknowledges that in 1976 (the year of Mao's death), "the Chinese people remained far from achieving the promises of socialism."[21] While tremendous industrial growth occurred during the Mao period, the authors also make clear that there were substantial problems in the organization of industrial production, resulting in declining productivity. There was overproduction of some goods and underproduction of others, inefficient transportation and distribution, and difficulties with poor product quality. Importantly, Hart-Landsberg and Burkett link these economic problems to wider social and political maladies. They acknowledge that the Chinese people did not exercise democratic control over their economic and political life, and that workers were "given little opportunity or encouragement to take control over the conditions of production."[22] Thus, the authors suggest that there was "a critical need to build on the strengths of China's past achievements while... enhanc[ing] the direct control of the associated producers over the conditions and products of their labor."[23]

Second, Hart-Landsberg and Burkett emphasize that China's capitalist restoration did not result from a single plenary session meeting, and that market reforms were not pursued, at least initially, out of capitalist greed. In fact, they place little emphasis on the Maoist "capitalist roader" rhetoric which even today is advanced by some left scholars—including Minqi Li, Mobo Gao, and the editors of *Monthly Review*—as a serious explanation for Deng's reform course.[24] Instead, they suggest that the 1978 decision to pursue "socialist modernization" was largely technical and administrative, aiming to resolve China's economic problems by "raising the country's productive forces and not further experimentation with new socialist relations of production."[25] However:

while it may have been a party decision to begin marketization, market imperatives quickly proved uncontrollable. Each stage in the reform process generated new tensions and contradictions that were resolved only through a further expansion of market power, leading to the growing consolidation of a capitalist political economy. Thus, rather than 'using capitalism to build socialism' as reformers argued would be the case, the reality has been that market socialism 'used socialism to build capitalism.'[26]

As market reforms increasingly alienated the Party from its working-class base, Party bureaucrats sought to restore private property as a mechanism for securing their privileges.[27] Taken as a whole, this is a compelling and innovative analysis of the contradictions of Chinese market socialism.

Despite these positive features, however, their alternative account of capitalist restoration has profound difficulties. First, Hart-Landsberg and Burkett do not identify when restoration actually took place. This is not simply an oversight—it reflects theoretical ambiguities underlying their entire work. Hart-Landsberg and Burkett identify 1) transformation of industrial structure and primitive accumulation; 2) widening societal polarization and working-class destitution; 3) increasing dependence on exports; and 4) overproduction and deflation as *indicators* of capitalism. However, only the first of these phenomena can be taken as a straightforward metric of restoration. The closest they come to identifying a point of qualitative transformation is in their discussion of China's obligations under the WTO and "normal trade relations" with the US, where they approvingly cite the observations of Hong Kong socialist Liu Yufan:

The agreement requires that 'SOEs [state-owned enterprises] and state investment firms will trade according to commercial principles, and the government will avoid influencing commercial decisions of SOEs.' It is no exaggeration to suggest that the WTO pledges not only 'imply the complete and irreversible destruction of the last remnants of the planned economy and the complete restoration of capitalism, but also amount to giving up substantial economic sovereignty to imperialism.'[28] [Quotations are Liu's]

It is highly questionable whether the Chinese government actually implemented this or other WTO measures that supposedly signalled "the complete restoration of capitalism." Hart-Landsberg and Burkett therefore leave readers with the implicit suggestion that capitalism was restored simply through the quantitative extension of market relations, and thereby ignore the crucial question of when quantity turned into *quality*. When did China transform from being a non-capitalist society *with* markets into an unmistakably capitalist society? Moreover, *how* was this achieved? Do markets possess their own imperatives (a "dynamic of their own") such that their introduction already contains the seed of capitalism?[29] Or do capitalist markets require social relations that are fundamentally distinct from those in non-capitalist societies that still possess markets? This question has analytical and a political implications. If Hart-Landsberg and Burkett want to maintain that China was *once* an alternative but now ceases to be, it is incumbent on them and all socialists addressing this issue to identify when capitalist restoration occurred, and what was truly decisive in this transformation.

Similarly, while Hart-Landsberg and Burkett are right to point out the contradictory dynamics inherent in market reforms, they do not address the important question of whether the "growing consolidation of a capitalist economy" could have been halted at any point. In speaking of capitalist restoration, they imply it was once possible that a redirection of state policies from above could have prevented capitalist tendencies, but that such a redirection is now impossible. At times the authors themselves employ language which suggests that a "full-fledged capitalist restoration" has not *yet* been achieved. For example, they refer to "the ongoing capitalization of China's economy" when analyzing the perils faced by Chinese workers, and to China's "increasingly bourgeois state" when discussing state repression of worker militancy.[30] But if the Chinese state is only "increasingly bourgeois," is it not yet bourgeois—or simply less bourgeois than other capitalist states? And if somehow less bourgeois, does this not mean that the PRC *can* act as an alternative to prevailing capitalist models, if only in a very limited sense? To be clear, the problem here is not the suggestion that capitalist restoration is a process rather than an event. Instead, the problem is that Hart-Landsberg and Burkett suggest that the process is at once ongoing *and* complete.

Hart-Landsberg and Burkett are not the only ones who are ambiguous on these questions. Robert Weil, another frequent contributor to *Monthly Review*, condemns "the emergence of a full-blown Chinese capitalism" in a 2006 piece detailing the plight of the contemporary Chinese working classes.[31] In another article appearing only a month later, Weil correctly savages Jung Chang and Jon Halliday's scurrilous biography of Mao.[32] In the course of doing so, however, Weil seems to suggest that Chinese capitalism may be less "full-blown":

> *Mao: The Unknown Story* must thus be understood as one salvo in the battle for the 'hearts and minds' of the Chinese people as they face a critical turning point, whether to plunge completely over the cliff of capitalist restoration and corporate 'globalization,' or to turn back from the precipice and begin to rebuild a society in which socialism and working classes have a meaningful role in determining the direction of official policy.[33]

It seems, then, that the legacy of Mao—and the broader principles of socialism with which he has been identified—are of political relevance today not because it may be harnessed to reverse an already existing "full-blown capitalism," but because it may be invoked to prevent a restoration *that is not yet complete.* This leads to a consideration the most important lacuna in the work of Hart-Landsberg and Burkett: the question of the state. Without an outline, much less an analysis, of the state form that emerged from the 1949 Revolution, the authors are unable to ground their tepid criticisms of Maoist China in a broader theoretical understanding of the contradictions that beset all bureaucratically planned economies. Consequently, a number of questions are left unanswered. Why did Deng choose to use market reforms as a means of improving the economy, rather than experimenting with "new socialist relations of production"? If the social base of the CCP was ever truly the working class, as Hart-Landsberg and Burkett maintain, how could capitalist restoration be pushed through without mass working class resistance? In their work, class struggle largely exists as a *future* prospect—a force that can reverse restoration if and when it finally exerts itself. But has class struggle not shaped the reform process in a profound way? And if so, might such struggle complicate the simple top-down narrative of capitalist restoration?

Finally, how have capitalist reforms affected the CCP itself? While it is certainly true that many Party officials welcomed privatization as a means of securing and expanding their privileges, it stands to reason that not all government officials, Party apparatchiks, and factory managers stood to win from the process. Are these elements simply too weak and marginal to effect any strong resistance to ongoing marketization processes? Should inter-bureaucratic factionalism have a bearing on our assessment of restoration? Does it matter that the CCP remains a Party for which Marxism supposedly provides "the fundamental guiding thought for the establishment of Party and state"?[34] Even if cynical, do these official commitments place a restraint on reforms? These are yet another set of questions that are crucial to an understanding of whether China can still act as an alternative. But to answer them we will need a more elaborated theoretical apparatus than that provided by Hart-Landsberg and Burkett.

Adam Smith in Beijing: Neo-Smithian *mea culpa*

At first glance it seems that Arrighi is much less concerned with the question of market socialism and its viability than Hart-Landsberg and Burkett. Although he is open to the possibility that Chinese socialism may be reinvigorated, Arrighi is explicit that what concerns him "is not so much the fate of the socialist tradition in China, as the broader implications of the Chinese ascent for inter-civilizational relations in the world at large."[35] In this, Arrighi remains true to his previous work in world systems theory, which was more concerned with the structures that reproduce international inequality than those that reproduce inequality within nations.[36] Military, diplomatic and exchange relations are given priority over production relations. It is probably for this reason that Arrighi recalled, in an interview published shortly before his death in 2009, that he was far less upset than his one-time collaborator John Saul over the failure of African socialism: "For me, these were national liberation movements; they were not in any way socialist movements, even when they embraced the rhetoric of socialism. They were populist regimes, and therefore I didn't expect much beyond national liberation, which we both saw as very important."[37] Yet, as Saul himself has recounted, Arrighi's apparent insouciance regarding socialism was more a product of latter-day political pessimism than a conviction confidently asserted at the time.[38] Indeed, when asked if his "commonwealth of civilizations" could be described as socialism, Arrighi replied that the latter had become outdated because of its historical identification with the state:

> [I]f this world system was going to be called socialist, it would need to be redefined in terms of a mutual respect between humans and a collective respect for nature. But this may have to be organized through state-regulated market exchanges, so as to empower labour and disempower capital in Smithian fashion, rather than through state ownership and control of the means of production.[39]

From Oskar Lange onward, market socialists have typically emphasized the necessity of some form of public ownership, recognizing it as the *sine qua non* of socialism itself. "Capital" can then be made to disappear because its indispensable prerequisite—private property—is absent. Yet market competition between firms is upheld as a necessary means of achieving "efficient allocation of resources," given the inefficiencies associated with the "soft budget constraint" of centrally planned economies.[40] The result, according to market socialists, is the best of both worlds: market competition produces increasing dividends rather than stagnation, but public ownership ensures that such dividends can be redistributed throughout society to serve social and political goals, rather than private profit.[41] Arrighi's vision overlaps with market socialism in treating the market as a mere "instrument of governance"; but differs by seeming to regard public ownership as unnecessary for achieving just social goals. Instead of capturing and redistributing profits produced by publicly-held enterprises, a more equal and just social order can be achieved by state regulation of market exchange, forcing capital to compete without degrading labor.

Arrighi therefore urges a reappraisal of Deng's reforms, suggesting that confusion surrounding them "is symptomatic of widespread misconceptions about the relationship between market economy, capitalism, and economic development."[42] To clarify these issues, he engages with a central question that has emerged in historical debates surrounding the "Great Divergence": why did Europe, rather than China, make the breakthrough to the Industrial Revolution? He agrees with Kenneth Pomeranz's suggestion that imperial China possessed sufficient commercialization to activate a genuinely "Smithian" dynamic: "A process of economic improvement driven by productivity gains attending a widening and deepening division of labor limited only by the extent of the market."[43] However, whereas Pomeranz suggests that European take-off was contingent on *surpassing* the limitations of typically Smithian growth, Arrighi avers that Smith actually identified two developmental paths: an "unnatural," foreign trade-based, energy- and capital-intensive path typical of Europe; and a "natural" or home trade-based, energy-saving and labor-intensive path typical of China.[44] Although Smith is routinely portrayed as a theorist and proponent of capitalist development, Arrighi suggests that he was no such thing. Rather than being an advocate of a minimalist state, Smith proposed a strong state that would regulate the market, intervene "to correct or counter its socially or politically undesirable outcomes," administer justice, fund national defence, and provide physical infrastructure and education.[45] Observing the tripartite class structure of England, Smith recognized that the interests of property owners were liable to clash with the "general interest" because they always involved a widening of the market a narrowing of competition. The task of government was therefore to "ensure that capitalists compete with one another in reducing profits to the bare minimum necessary to compensate for the risks of investing resources in trade and production." Legislators should countervail the monopoly power of merchants and manufacturers.[46]

With this peculiar reading of Smith, Arrighi is able to redeploy his distinctly "Braudelian" understanding of capitalism as the "top layer of the hierarchy of world trade," constituting a monopolistic anti-market distinguishable from the market economy and material life.[47] The origins of the Great Divergence do not lie in the fortuitous circumstances of the early nineteenth century, but in the much earlier capture of European states by capitalists:

> [T]he feature that enables us to distinguish between the European and East Asian market-based development paths is not the presence of particular governmental and business institutions as such, but their combination in different power structures. Thus, [Adam] Smith's 'unnatural' path differs from the 'natural,' not because it has a larger number of capitalists, but because capitalists have greater power to impose their class interest at the expense of the national interest. In Marx's reconceptualization of Smith's unnatural path as the 'capitalist' path, this greater power has turned governments into committees for managing the affairs of the bourgeoisie.[48]

Capitalist conquest of state power in Europe enabled the use of imperialist practices in the pursuit of long-distance trade and high finance, establishing a synergy between capital and power. Inter-state competition for mobile capital inaugurated an historical sequence of declining and emerging capitalist powers, with each new power acting as larger "containers" for material accumulation. For Arrighi, "it is this *sequence* of endless accumulation of capital and power, more than anything else, that defines the European developmental path as 'capitalist.'" On the one hand, it is a narrative that accords with Marx's discussion in *Capital* of the credit system facilitating "different moments of primitive accumulation."[49] At the same time, however, Arrighi insists that it answers a central lacuna in Marx: *why* capitalist agencies are driven to accumulate money for its own sake. Accumulation is not merely an economic activity, but is fully imbricated in processes of military and political competition— with control of the world's financial resources providing decisive advantage in the control of all other resources. It is therefore entirely misleading, according to Arrighi, to seek the origins of capitalism in agriculture, as some Marxists (e.g., Robert Brenner) have done; instead, the bourgeoisie originated in foreign, long-distance trade.[50] Indeed, capitalism "nearly occurred first" in Song China around 1300; some of China's coastal merchants resembled their Dutch counterparts in wealth and power. Yet they ultimately failed to subordinate the state to their own interests, and became increasingly constrained by Beijing's "inward-looking" policies in subsequent centuries.[51]

The question of "Who controls the state?" is therefore central to Arrighi's political economy generally, and his estimation of the PRC specifically.[52] Since foreign investment has only been welcomed "on terms and conditions that suit China's national interest," the government can in no way be characterized as a servant of foreign or diasporic Chinese capitalist interests. However, Arrighi is uncertain whether a national bourgeoisie has come into existence and, if it has, whether it has succeeded in "seizing control of the commanding heights of Chinese economy and society."[53] Such hesitancy is warranted because it is not at all clear, given Arrighi's analysis of capitalism, how we might know when and if capitalist interests have triumphed over the vaguely conceived national interest. There thus emerges a bifurcation in Arrighi's analysis of China, revealing the profound limitations and contradictions of his framework.

Consistent with his overall analysis, Arrighi suggests that a central Smithian feature of China's transition

is the government's active encouragement of competition, not just among foreign capitals, but among all capitals, whether foreign or domestic, private or public. Indeed, the reforms put greater emphasis on the intensification of competition through the breakup of national monopolies and the elimination of barriers, than on privatization. The result has been a constant over-accumulation of capital and downward pressure on rates of profits, which has been characterized as China's "jungle capitalism" but looks more like a Smithian world of capitalists driven by relentless competition to work in the national interest.[54]

This should be enough evidence to confidently assert that China's political economy remains robustly non-capitalist. Yet the unspoken assumption is that "relentless" competition among capitalists has somehow served the "national interest"—a realist concept that, as Leo Panitch has noted, completely obscures "the increasingly unequal class-society that China has become."[55] Arrighi is aware of these divisions, however, which is perhaps why he turns to a different metric for assessing China's capitalist character: primitive accumulation, or David Harvey's "accumulation by dispossession."[56] Instead of seeking the origins of capitalism and capitalists in foreign trade and international credit cycles, Arrighi now places the transformation of domestic relations of production and exploitation front and center. In making this shift, he begins to offer a more serious case for China's status as a "non-capitalist market society."

In this context Arrighi returns to a point made earlier in his analysis but never reconciled with his world systems approach. Echoing Samir Amin, Arrighi maintains that "as long as the principle of equal access to land continues to be recognized and implemented, it is not too late for social action in contemporary China to steer evolution in a non-capitalist direction."[57] Much of China's economic growth during the reform period, it turns out, relied upon collective ownership forms in rural areas: peasants retained use rights to land under the "Household Responsibility

System," while collective ownership of the burgeoning township and villages enterprises (TVEs) ensured the reinvestment of profits to meet local social and welfare aims.[58] The SOEs, in addition, were increasingly subject to pressures of market competition but not to a Russian-style privatization.[59] Nevertheless, Deng's reforms have created myriad opportunities for Party cadres, government officials and SOE managers to engage in various forms of accumulation by dispossession, gathering huge fortunes through the appropriation of public property, embezzlement of state funds, and sale of land use rights. It is this tussle between tendencies of accumulation without dispossession and accumulation with dispossession that defines the contours of Chinese politics. Under the regime of Jiang Zemin (1989-2002), the latter tendency seemed poised to triumph. However, the escalation of social protest prompted Hu Jintao (2002-2012) to implement policies that have stemmed the tide.[60]

While expressing admiration for the CCP's "mass line" and "two-way socialization" traditions, Arrighi admits that in recent years they have largely applied to relations between the party-state and the emerging bourgeoisie rather than the subaltern classes.[61] Still, as the Chinese New Left scholar Wang Hui has suggested, the fact that the Chinese Revolution and socialist ideology have not been repudiated is of tremendous importance. On the one hand, the socialist tradition functions as an internal restraint on reforms, such that every major policy shift must be conducted in dialogue with it. On the other hand, the tradition invests workers and peasants with a legitimate discourse for challenging their dispossession, shaping what is possible for future political struggles.[62]

Overall, Arrighi's work draws attention to several important issues neglected by Hart-Landsberg and Burkett. Most central are the social relations of agriculture, which receive scant and erroneous treatment in *China and Socialism*.[63] Collective ownership in the countryside (affecting land use rights and TVEs), and state control of enterprises may constitute enduring gains from the Chinese Revolution and provide a plausible basis for assessing China as a non-capitalist alternative. Arrighi is also right to suggest, against received wisdom in almost all corners, that the socialist traditions of the CCP and PRC are not simply hollow and cynical, but also serve as resources in struggles over the conditions and terms of reproduction. In that sense, they are very material.

Yet, it is also clear that if these insights are to be given greater consideration within historical materialist debates, they must be extricated from the rotten shell of world systems theory. Reading Smith through a Braudelian lens, Arrighi directly confronts a number of central questions that are left vague or entirely unasked in the work of Hart-Landsberg and Burkett: What defines capitalism and the capitalist state? Are markets distinct from capitalism? Can there be non-capitalist market societies? But asking the right questions is not enough. The fact that Arrighi applauds *both* the protests of laid-off SOE workers *and* the competitive market pressures that engendered such lay-offs exposes the profound limitations of his Braudelian conception of capitalism.

Arrighi's assessment of the Chinese Revolution, the planned economy, and the motivations of Deng's reforms are even more limited than that of Hart-Landsberg and Burkett. The CCP and the revolution it led are valorized chiefly for having mobilized peasants in the countryside, with little acknowledgement of the anti-democratic form this mobilization took and even less recognition of the problems it created for the Party's relationship with the urban working class—the ostensible "vanguard" of the revolution.[64] The differing national and international policies of Mao and Deng are portrayed as pragmatic reactions to the prevailing winds of the Cold War. The CCP was supposedly driven to use ideology as the "main weapon in the struggle to consolidate its power nationally and internationally" as long as it was cut off from global trade; but when the weapon backfired during the Cultural Revolution and the US extended its hand, the stage was set for a turn to the market.[65] This narrative usefully highlights the international and geopolitical dimensions of Beijing's political economic calculation (something neglected by Hart-Landsberg and Burkett)—but it also ignores the contradictions of the bureaucratically-planned economy and the class dimensions of Chinese decision making. Without these, no comprehensive understanding of the reform process and contemporary Chinese political economy can be achieved.

Considered comparatively, *China and Socialism* and *Adam Smith in Beijing* paint strikingly different portraits of contemporary China. Hart-Landsberg and Burkett argue that the market reforms instituted by Deng, while not instantly restoring capitalism, set in motion a process that culminated in a full-fledged capitalist restoration. Not only have the reforms led to dispossession and increasing hardship for Chinese workers, they have also made the country's development increasingly dependent upon foreign investment and demand. Arrighi, in sharp contrast, maintains that Chinese development has, thus far, followed a distinctly non-capitalist path even while being very much market-oriented. Although tendencies of accumulation by dispossession have been strong and at times dominant, they have not yet overwhelmed accumulation *without* dispossession (predicated especially upon access to land). Not only has China's developmental model been strongly inward-oriented, if maintained and strengthened it may yet facilitate a reorientation of global resource flows away from the imperialist North to anchor a new world market society "truly respectful of cultural differences."[66] Neither work, however, fully succeeds in making its case. It is necessary to ask, then, what should be adopted and what should be rejected in seeking to clarify China's status as a non-capitalist alternative?

Arrighi asks many of the right questions. While his search for a "non-capitalist market economy" derives from historical pessimism about the prospects for socialism, Arrighi is still correct to suggest that confusion and imprecision pervades much Marxist writing about the relationship between the market economy and capitalism. Hart-Landsberg and Burkett, for example, imply that markets contain an inherently capitalist logic, such that capitalist restoration follows inevitably from their unchecked development. Asking questions about markets in pre-capitalist societies can help to sharpen an historical materialist understanding of the specificity of capitalist markets. At the same time, Arrighi's glorification of market *competition*, and consequent disregard of the capital-labor relation, provides little enlightenment. His own belated recognition of the importance of primitive accumulation suggests as much. Hart-Landsberg and Burkett are therefore quite correct to draw a link between market competition and primitive accumulation, even if, as Arrighi suggests, they understate the extent to which accumulation without dispossession remains important. Adequately addressing this empirical question, then, requires an elaboration and clarification of its theoretical significance. A clearer specification of the central categories left vague or misunderstood in both works—capitalism and the capitalist state—also opens the door to a more sophisticated assessment of Mao's bureaucratic "socialism." *China and Socialism* and *Adam Smith in Beijing* provide only cursory analyses of this social form, an understanding of which is crucial to grasping the reform process and contemporary realities.

Chapter Three

Clarifying Capitalism: How is it a Unique Social Form?

At a glance, there would seem to be little that is common in the concepts of capitalism advanced by Hart-Landsberg and Burkett, on the one hand, and Arrighi, on the other. On closer inspection, though, it is possible to identify a shared problem: an *ahistorical* conception of capitalism, capitalists and markets. This claim may appear absurd. An historical understanding of capitalism is supposed to be the very hallmark of the Marxist approach advanced by Hart-Landsberg and Burkett. And Arrighi expends great analytical effort distinguishing capitalist and non-capitalist market societies, utilizing Marx as well as Braudel. But this also raises a huge hurdle, because Marx's work hardly provides a single, coherent account of how capitalism arose and what made it a truly unique social form. Arrighi pivots between two aspects of primitive accumulation outlined in *Capital*: dispossession, on the one hand, and the credit system, on the other. Each implies quite different understandings of capitalist dynamics. The point for our analysis is not to locate the "true" Marx, for he is unlikely to be found. The task instead is to identify how Marx's distinct and even contradictory accounts of capitalism have compelled contemporary Marxist scholars to adopt differing and incompatible methodological strategies. It then becomes possible to seek a way out of the impasse by identifying, clarifying, and expanding those aspects of Marx's account that are most illuminating, while rejecting those that ultimately serve as barriers to understanding.

As an entry point for this discussion it is useful to reproduce at length two assessments of the Marxism found in *China and Socialism* and *Adam Smith in Beijing*. Participating in an early debate on Hart-Landsberg and Burkett's work, Alvin So remarked:

> The structural contradiction of capital and labour in production relations, upon which Hart-Landsberg and Burkett base their argument, is discussed at a high level of abstraction and is taken to be universally applicable to every capitalist society. What is overlooked in this mode of analysis, however, is historical specificity, i.e., how the logic of capital actually works itself out in a concrete historical setting and is embedded with specific national traits. In the Chinese historical context, for example, market reforms emerged in a context in which the party-state directly controlled almost every aspect of the economy and society. Thus, it is crucial to bring the *state* back in to examine the historical development of China.[1]

Hart-Landsberg and Burkett are not alone among Marxists in simplistically applying abstract models derived from *Capital*, and are hardly the worst offenders. It is quite typical of Marxist economists to define capitalism as a system of "generalized commodity production," thereby establishing an analytical basis for the abstract analysis of the capitalist law of value but avoiding altogether the question of its historical origin.[2]

How should historical specificity and the role of the state be brought back in? What deficiencies do they need to correct? Richard Walker—a Marxist scholar who has contributed insightful work on primitive accumulation in contemporary China[3]—suggests that *Adam Smith in Beijing*, despite many flaws, provides useful insights:

> Returning to the failure of China to make the great leap into modern industry, what was lacking? ... They certainly developed their economies to a high degree on a Smithian

basis. But it is equally indisputable that, in the end, China and the others did not undergo the same degree of penetration and expansion of commodity-exchange, the same revolutionary transformation of production, or explosive extroversion as Europe....

In [imperial] China, the ability of the state to suppress the merchant-class and their expansionary tendencies appears to have been critical to that country's involution. On this point, Arrighi's statist view of politics complements the Marxist model of class struggle. The Ming Dynasty was obsessed with danger from the north and the Mongol Qings put an end to the autonomy of the southern merchants—although the state's ability to defeat the merchants surely depended on the latter's relative weakness in the overall social order, unlike the English merchants who helped oust the Stuart kings in the seventeenth century.[4]

For Walker, the role of the state helps to reconcile the good and the bad in Arrighi's work. On the one hand, Walker is impressed by what the world-systems school "has right": long-distance trade, the world market, and the inter-imperial, coercive and hegemonic form of politics they engender. On the other hand, he objects to Arrighi's dismissal of dispossession as a necessary corollary of capitalist production.[5] His solution is to emphasize the peculiarly expansive nature of the European "commodity revolution"—one that failed to take off in China because merchants never grabbed hold of the state. Arrighi's ability to harmonize Marx and Weber, therefore, seems to reside in bringing us back to the concept of bourgeois revolution, a familiar tenet of nineteenth-century political thought. In reality, however, this resolution only reproduces the schizophrenic quality of *Adam Smith in Beijing*.

Two models of capitalist transition

To overcome models of abstract polarization and bourgeois revolution, it is necessary to trace their roots in Marx's own work by returning to insights offered by the transition debate. After all, it was with the goal of explaining the emergence of a system of free wage labor and generalized commodity production that Marxists initially turned their attention to the historical question of capitalism's origins, naturally drawing inspiration from the writings of Marx himself. The problem, as Robert Brenner initially pointed out, is that Marx seems to offer two *distinct* accounts of the transition; moreover, on closer inspection, the two are not merely distinct but *mutually incompatible*.[6] The first (hereafter "model one"), presented in Marx's early works, poses a theory of historical development based on a relatively linear progression through different modes of production, propelled by a tension between the forces and relations of production. Although the exact constitution of the productive forces is disputed, in these early works Marx seems to suggest that the division of labor directly expresses the level of development of the productive forces; *evolves in response to the expanding market*; and determines, in turn, the social relations of class and property.[7] Notice here the crucial role that the expanding market plays as a motive force in Marx's overall conception of historical development.

Within the premises of model one, the West European bourgeois revolutions are represented as but the latest example of the dynamic productive forces (urban bourgeoisie) bursting asunder "outmoded" (feudal) relations of production.[8] Although considerably finessed, the work of Perry Anderson offers a largely similar account, portraying towns, market trading, and the revival of Roman law and quiritary property ownership as inherently antagonistic to feudal social relations.[9] An emphasis on the causal importance of trade and towns is also a hallmark of

Paul Sweezy's work,[10] which was later elaborated and extended by the world-systems theorists. They, like Arrighi, understand the emergence of capitalism as a much more temporally and geographically extended process, predicated upon the metropolitan bourgeoisie's exploitation of the periphery through mercantilism and colonialism. Various forms of coerced labor and generalized violence are given prominence as aspects of primitive accumulation that historically precede industrialization and generalized wage labor.

For Brenner and the "political Marxists,|" the problem with this account lies in its assumption of what actually needs to be explained—*viz.*, specifically capitalist "rules of reproduction" and "laws of motion." Brenner points out that Adam Smith's *description* of capitalism's dynamic is largely correct. Market competition induces actors to cut costs by innovating and improving labor productivity, leading to a more specialized technical division of labor. However, Smith is only able to describe this dynamic by assuming the causal priority of an intrinsically human capitalist rationality—the propensity to "truck, barter, and exchange."[11] This propensity is also assumed by Arrighi, who suggests that capitalists, as profit-maximizing agents, already existed within the interstices of pre-capitalist societies, whether European or East Asian.[12] Since merchants have been trading for centuries and millennia, capitalism—despite the importance ascribed to bourgeois revolution—is effectively conceived as merely a quantitative extension of social relations that have always been present. Its emergence at a particular time is therefore attributed to the removal of barriers or obstacles in its path (guild and feudal restrictions, non-capitalist state officials, etc.), rather than to qualitatively new social behaviors.

Even prominent British Marxist historians like Rodney Hilton and Maurice Dobb exhibit the same explanatory tendency, which Ellen Wood refers to as the "commercialization model" of the transition. While appropriately focusing on the peasantry and rural social relations, they root the emergence of capitalism and a waged proletariat in the process of peasant differentiation and polarization. With the Black Plague and loosening of lordly exploitation in medieval Western Europe, it is claimed, rich peasants were in a better position to take advantage of potential "gains from trade" offered by an expanding market, while their poorer counterparts—those less able to produce and market competitively—fell even further behind. The differential effects of market competition eventually resulted in a polarization between capitalist farmers on the one hand and landless laborers on the other.[13] The affinities between this polarization model of transition and the one offered by Hart-Landsberg and Burkett are apparent.

Political Marxists contrast the "commercialization model" with a second model drawn from parts of Marx's *Capital*. In his famous chapter on "so-called primitive accumulation," Marx does not trace capitalism to the lifting of barriers to profit-making, but rather to the forcible expropriation of the peasantry from customary lands through enclosure.[14] The separation of the direct producers from their means of subsistence is therefore the original "primitive accumulation," not the accumulation of wealth via colonialism or trade. However, Marx's account did not adequately explain the historical reasons for this expropriation. If we are not to assume a capitalist rationality from the outset, how do we explain *why* feudal landlords sought to expel the peasantry from their land? Did a similar process occur outside of England, and if not, how are these societies to be characterized during the same historical period?

English origins of the capital relation

Brenner sought to answer these questions in his famously controversial essay on early modern Europe, which provided a foundation for political Marxism.[15] In doing so he offered the first explanation of capitalism that did not confuse *explanans* with *explanandum*. Rather than conceiving of historical change in terms of a dialectic between the forces and relations of production, Brenner instead points to the radical difference between capitalism and all previous forms of class-stratified society. While technique, organization and technology have varied across time and place, in all pre-capitalist societies the production of goods assumed a basically similar form. Peasants cultivated the land they held in some manner of direct possession, but not *ownership* in the contemporary capitalist sense. Surplus appropriation (and therefore class exploitation) did not generally occur at the point of production as it does in capitalist societies, but instead through the exercise of political power and implicit coercion after the agricultural product had been cultivated. In pre-capitalist class societies, therefore, political and economic powers were fused and in fact indistinguishable. Modes of production (or modes of exploitation as they have also been called) are then meaningfully distinguished from each other by their form of "social property relations," which Brenner defines as

> the relations among direct producers, relations among exploiters, and relations between exploiters and direct producers that, taken together, make possible/specify the regular access of individuals and families to the means of production (land, labour, tools) and/or the social product *per se*. The idea is that such relations will exist in every society, and define the basic constraints on—and the possibilities and limits of—individual economic action.[16]

In this light, accounting for the transition to capitalism means explaining how it was possible at all. Why would lords enclose on the direct producers who provide their wealth and security? Brenner's answer, which has been given important elaboration by

Comninel,[17] is that capitalism emerged as an *unintended conse-quence* of class struggles in England specifically. The Black Death (c. 1348) and consequent depopulation affected most of Western Europe, jeopardizing the normal "rules of reproduction" that had once governed lordly accumulation. In France, peasant communities were able to secure rights of inheritance and fixed rents against their lords, even as new powers of politically-mediated appropriation were being formed by tax-office absolutist states.[18] The rights of taxation, trade and legislation were held as the personal property of the ruling dynast,[19] and private appropriation was secured through obtaining politically-constituted property, specifically state offices. Thus, interna-tional politics, and ultimately warfare, was instrumental to the reproduction of absolutist ruling classes, who depended on violence to control mercantilist sea lanes and to tax new peasant populations. Contra Arrighi, mercantilist long-distance trade and monopolies were products of pre-capitalist, not capitalist, rules of reproduction.

In England, though, a very different path was followed. Here, depopulation also turned the terms of class struggle against lords, and attempts to re-impose feudal exactions failed.[20] Whereas serfs were once obliged to perform a certain amount of labor upon the lords' *demesne*, they were now relieved of labor-rent obligations and obliged to only pay money rents on their customary tenancies.[21] This peasant victory set into motion a series of interconnected events that eventually yielded agrarian capitalism. Lacking extra-economic powers of surplus extraction, in the mid-fifteenth century the lords began to rent their *demesne* land to the highest bidder, i.e., they established variable "economic" rents. Although this would otherwise have had no consequence for customary tenants, the English common law (absent in France) enabled the lords to claim *exclusive* right to common lands. There began a process—largely "legal"—by which common lands and rights were extinguished, and lords increasingly asserted their right to enact variable rents on customary holdings as well.[22] Peasant access to the means of subsistence (land) became conditional upon meeting a market-determined rent. For tenants, production for the market was now an *imperative*, rather than an opportunity—they had to specialize, innovate, and improve productivity just to ensure their self-reproduction. Those who failed to do so sufficiently were evicted, and came to constitute a wage-dependent proletariat. This result differed markedly from that in France, where enduring peasant possession of land ensured the maintenance of pre-capitalist rules of reproduction. A secular tendency of declining labor productivity set in as peasant families subdivided their holdings over the generations. To subsist, many peasant families necessarily *supplemented* their income with wages and "proto-industrial" production; but "[t]enant faming and wage labor had changed little since the crisis of the fourteenth century... whereas capitalism had totally transformed the agriculture of England."[23]

The state and the global diffusion of capitalist imperatives

To summarize, political Marxists have offered at least two fundamental contributions to our understanding of the relationship between capitalism, the market, and the state. The first is identifying capitalism's specificity. Their analysis has shown that it is at least misleading to begin with an abstract capitalist mode of production predicated upon free wage labor. Instead, market dependence is the historical basis for capitalist development, upon which proletarianization followed. As Wood suggests:

The moment access to the means of production and appropriation becomes market-dependent—and even before market dependence takes the form of the general commodification of labour power—the 'fundamental contradiction' of capitalism is already at work, and the market's imperatives of competition and profit-maximization come into play.[24]

Second, the capital relation emerged not though an urban bourgeoisie conquering state power, but through a transformation in the form of the state and political power itself. In assessing a state's capitalist character, then, the operative question is not who *controls* the state, but what the state *does*. In fact, if we were to focus on those states that conform most closely to Arrighi's understanding of "committees" instrumentally ruled by those making profits through foreign trade—the Italian city-states and Holland—it is precisely their dependence on extra-economic superiority, especially in shipping and military technology, that distinguish them as *non-capitalist*.[25] It is only when the political and economic spheres are separated that the capital relation is obtained, because this institutionally insulates the "market" from the "state" and thereby compels relations of market dependence. The autonomous political form of the capitalist state is itself a relation of production.[26]

Conceiving of the capitalist state in this way shifts historical materialist concern from instrumental control to the question of capitalists' structural power vis-à-vis the state, given their direct role in accumulation and investment. As Leo Panitch suggests:

It is in these terms that we should conceptualize the "relative autonomy" of the capitalist state: not as being autonomous from capitalist classes or the economy, but rather in having capacities to act on behalf of the system as a whole (autonomy), while their dependence on the success of overall accumulation for their own legitimacy and reproduction nevertheless leaves these capacities bounded (relative).[27]

At the same time, the historically-informed approach to understanding the capitalist state outlined above also guards against the type of functional analyses often undertaken by structuralist Marxist state theorists.[28] State policies that cannot be ascribed to the instrumental demands of specific class fractions are instead explained as being undertaken on behalf of the "system as a whole." This places analytical emphasis on structural reproduction of the capital relation, rather than the open-ended historical process through which the relation itself is contested and challenged in the course of being reproduced.[29]

The analytical shift from structure to historical process (what E.P. Thompson termed "structured process")[30] is all the more important when we consider the combined and uneven nature in which capitalism has developed globally in the past two centuries. For if capitalism originally emerged in England as an unintended consequence of agrarian class struggle, its subsequent institution in Western Europe and beyond was often very much *intended*. In this sense, Arrighi is correct to criticize Marx's prediction that the spread of capitalism would be a simple economic process, whereby "The cheap prices of its commodities are the heavy artillery with which [the bourgeoisie] batters down all Chinese walls."[31] As Benno Teschke has noted, the spread of capitalism

> was a *political* and, *a fortiori, geopolitical* process in which pre-capitalist state classes had to design counterstrategies of reproduction to defend their position in an international environment which put them at an economic *and* coercive disadvantage. More often than not, it was heavy artillery that battered down pre-capitalist walls, and the construction and reconstruction of these walls required new state strategies of modernization.[32]

The strategies employed were highly heterogeneous in both time and place. Not only did pre-capitalist state classes have to manage the highly conflictual process of forcing market-dependent strategies of reproduction on direct producers, they also had to ensure the maintenance of their own privileges even as their claim to surplus via politically-constituted property was being eroded. The strategies included the build-up of repressive state apparatuses with military and fiscal mobilization, neo-mercantilism and imperialism, and more anodyne liberal economic policies. In the course of the late nineteenth and early twentieth centuries, however, a radical counterstrategy of modernization also emerged to gain tremendous social support and state implementation: socialism.[33]

Chapter Four

Returning to Socialist 'Transition': Plan, Market and Bureaucracy

The previous chapter's analysis of capitalism as a system of social property relations based on market dependence, and the associated concept of uneven and combined development,[1] provide important intellectual tools for clarifying the nature of socialism in general, and the experience of Chinese socialism in particular.

Markets and planning in socialism

The first important point concerns the theory of market socialism. Market socialism gained particular attraction in the post-Soviet period as a strategy for combining the redistributive benefits of public ownership with the efficiencies of the market. In the political Marxist understanding, however, there is nothing inherently efficient about markets, at least if efficiency is equated with cost-cutting, profit-maximization, and productive reinvestment. Such efficiencies are obtained only in capitalist markets, i.e., those in which the basic necessities of life are produced for profitable exchange, and access to the means of subsistence is therefore market dependent. Insofar as a socialist society seeks to use markets for the specific purpose of obtaining capitalist-style efficiency gains, it is caught in an insoluble contradiction. On the one hand, to the extent that market efficiency is to be obtained, its *discipline* must be exerted; and for its discipline to be exerted, workers—even as "owners" of the means of production—must be compelled to compete and accumulate (i.e., exploit themselves) on pain of bankruptcy, dispossession or unemployment.[2] Such outcomes militate against the spirit if not the letter of public ownership. On the other hand, to the extent that a socialist public authority seeks to prevent the socially deleterious effects of market competition, it is compelled to curtail market discipline by using the powers of public ownership to maintain employment and prop up unprofitable state-owned enterprises. Ellen Wood is therefore quite correct to maintain that "market socialism is a contradiction in terms"[3]— but attempts to implement market socialism on the ground entail their own, real contradictions, and it may take some time before they are resolved in one direction or the other.

Does this mean, then, that capitalism is the surest vehicle for delivering gains in productivity and human living standards; and that socialism, to the extent that it relies upon planning, is destined to foster stagnation and inefficiency? If so, we would certainly have to concede that socialism, in its Marxist variant at least, is impossible. As David McNally has lucidly outlined:

> Central to the Marxian conception of socialism is the idea that it is possible to "defetishize" economic life, to free human beings from subjection to impersonal economic laws, to organize the production of goods and services according to a conscious plan rather than through the blind workings of the market....
>
> From this principle [of workers' struggles to maximize "free time"] flows the basic dynamic of a socialist economy, its tendency to develop the forces of production not in order to produce surplus value, but in order to reduce the amount of necessary social labour performed by its members.[4]

Abundance is therefore an essential condition for achieving the "all-round development of the individual" and realizing the famous principle of what Marx called the "higher phase of communist society": "From each according to his ability, to each according to his needs!"[5] It follows, then, that a transition from capitalist society to communism requires a dramatic increase in labor productivity, both to ensure a decent and secure level of provision of material goods and services, and time away from labor, "time for the free intellectual and social activity of the individual."[6]

But how is such a high degree of productivity to be achieved, if not through the disciplining mechanisms associated with the capitalist market? Why did economic planning in "state socialist" societies manifestly fail in achieving such ends? There are at least two important factors that must be highlighted. The first is the material prerequisites that Marx and Engels assumed successful revolutionary movements would inherit upon establishing workers' states. As Robin Blackburn has noted:

> In *The Communist Manifesto* and in other writings, Marx and Engels famously insisted that a genuine socialism could only be built on the basis already laid by capitalism; in *The German Ideology* they had observed that socialism would require social overturns in at least several of the most developed countries. From this classic Marxist conviction it followed that it was a complete delusion to attempt to "build socialism" in one large backward country, or, as was subsequently to be attempted, in a string of backward countries.[7]

That socialism could only be achieved on the basis of the productive forces established in advanced capitalist countries was accepted as common wisdom in the Second International, and was one of the reasons why the Russian Mensheviks, wedded to Marx's stage theory of history, advocated a bourgeois revolution and rejected the October Revolution.[8] Others, such as Leon Trotsky and his supporters, took a different tack: they adamantly supported the October Revolution, but warned that the Stalinists' abandonment of world revolution would not only make the achievement of socialism in Russia impossible, it would greatly augment the dangers of capitalist restoration.[9]

The second factor is the institutional forms required to successfully achieve transition. A workers' state confronts serious policy tensions, principally between providing a decent and secure standard of living for all on the one hand, and delivering more free time to working people on the other. In a short-term macroeconomic perspective, this tension is negotiated by determining an optimal balance between the structure of social consumption and the rate and direction of investment, implemented through an economic plan.[10] In the longer term, such tensions can only be overcome, or met with equal adequacy, by enhancing labor productivity. Socialist scholars have argued persuasively that institutions of workers' democracy—workers' councils composed of elected delegates—can greatly facilitate both economic planning at the macro level and labor-saving, quality-preserving innovations at the micro level. The late Ernest Mandel, for example, outlined a system of "democratically centralized planning and self management," in which democratically elected national congresses would establish a coherent general plan of economic production to be implemented by self-managing congresses of workers' councils in every economic sector.[11] McNally advocates a broadly similar system, suggesting that the mass participation of direct producers would enable a democratically established scale of social priorities, while providing opportunities and incentives for innovations in production.[12] It is worth noting that markets need not disappear entirely in such a transitional society. Both McNally and Mandel, and Trotsky before them, envisaged an interaction of plan, market, and workers' councils.[13] The long-term objective, however, would be to reduce the role of the market in resource allocation, and the market would not serve as the regulator of the economy as it does in capitalism and in theoretical models of market socialism.[14]

'State socialism' and the working class: The Chinese experience

The "state socialist" societies of the twentieth century, including China, fell short on both factors: neither inheriting the productive forces of advanced capitalism nor establishing enduring institutions of workers' democracy. This outcome, however, was not inevitable. As Gregor Benton has documented, there were tremendous political struggles within the Chinese Communist Party specifically, and the Chinese communist movement more generally, over a number of questions of pivotal importance: democracy within the Party; the centrality of workers' as against peasants' struggles; the necessity of passing through a distinct "bourgeois-democratic" stage of revolution; and the "revolutionary" status of the national bourgeoisie.[15] Particularly important was the period immediately following the April 1927 Shanghai massacre, in which thousands of Communists, trade unionists and militant students were murdered by the military forces of Chiang Kai-shek's Guomindang (GMD), a nationalist party backed by property-owning classes.

The significance of this event is routinely misunderstood by mainstream China scholars and critical writers alike. Arrighi, for example, suggests the massacre demonstrated that "the coastal regions where the bulk of the urban proletariat was concentrated were far too treacherous a ground from which to challenge foreign domination and the GMD's hegemony over the Chinese bourgeoisie."[16] In fact, the most important question posed was not whether the vanguard of the revolution would be found in the cities or the countryside, but whether the nationalist GMD and national bourgeoisie represented an ally or an enemy for direct producers. In 1924, the Communist International directed the CCP to enter into an alliance with the GMD (later rechristened as a "bloc of four classes" embracing workers, peasants, national bourgeoisie and petty bourgeoisie) for the broader goal of achieving a "bourgeois-democratic" revolution.[17] Yet, as Lucien Bianco has noted, "During the summer of 1926… it was the CCP, which organized 1,200,000 workers and 800,000 peasants, rather than the Kuomintang [GMD], that really ran the workers' and peasants' movement."[18] But in order to maintain the alliance dictated by the Kremlin's stage theory and narrow diplomatic interests, the CCP was directed to dampen social struggle in the countryside as well as the cities, discouraging the formation of soviets (councils) among workers and peasants alike.[19]

The tragedy of 1927 was, above all, a product of the suicidal class alliances dictated by rigid adherence to a stage-ist model of revolution. Events in China prompted Trotsky to extend his theory of permanent revolution and uneven and combined development,[20] which were then adopted by a number of important CCP members. These dissidents were hounded from the Chinese Party, as was Trotsky from the Russian. Under Mao's leadership, the CCP largely abandoned the cities but *retained* the two-stage theory of revolution, seeking an alliance with the "national" bourgeoisie in a "New Democracy." The "soviets" it formed in the countryside had none of the autonomy and democracy enjoyed by the early Russian soviets; the Party became more bureaucratized during the Yan'an period, despite prevailing mythology; and social struggles in the rural base areas were heavily policed and discouraged in order to maintain the support of the "patriotic" landlords and the GMD as "Second United Front" partners.[21]

The alliance with the GMD proved unsustainable after World War II, largely because of Chiang Kai-Shek's determination to wipe out the Communists once and for all. In the end, his thoroughly corrupt, parasitic, and demoralized forces proved unequal to the task, and the CCP's peasant-based army units swept into the cities from 1948 onwards, culminating in Mao's declaration of the People's Republic in Beijing on 1 October

1949.[22] As late as June 1949 Mao continued to advocate an extended period of capitalist development in post-revolutionary China, expressing the same broad spirit of Arrighi's writing:

> To counter imperialist oppression and to raise her backward economy to a higher level, China must utilize all the factors of urban and rural capitalism that are beneficial and not harmful to the national economy and people's livelihood; and we must unite with the national bourgeoisie in common struggle. Our present policy is to regulate capitalism, not to destroy it. But the national bourgeoisie cannot be the leader of the revolution, nor should it have the chief role in state power.[23]

Given the CCP's broad support for capitalist development, its neglect of urban struggle, and its repression of autonomous proletarian organizing, it is hardly surprising that it confronted the working class as an alien force upon its victorious return to the cities.[24] Its initial program was one of labor discipline and class collaboration, rather than workers' power—asserting its political monopoly against the class it claimed to represent.[25]

Initially, at least, it did seem as though the Party would follow through on its plans to implement a New Democratic capitalism. Many non-Communists were given high positions and titles within the new state. While these were largely decorative and ceremonial they served concrete purposes: enlisting the support of non-Communist Chinese for a national cause; reassuring private entrepreneurs and the technical intelligentsia that capitalist enterprises would be allowed to exist; and giving some credence to the claim that the new state rested on an alliance of four classes constituting "the people."[26] Indeed, while banks, industries and large commercial organizations once run by the GMD were expropriated, the number of privately owned industrial firms actually increased during the early years of Communist rule, accounting for nearly 40 percent of industrial output by 1953. Still, the private sector operated under strict regulations regarding prices, wages, working conditions and profits.[27] In the countryside, meanwhile, the landlords were eliminated as a class, and land redistributed to landless and land-poor peasants. As land titles were issued by the government, the land itself was effectively nationalized; yet the titles themselves could be bought, sold and mortgaged by their possessors.[28]

Yet this period of New Democracy proved fleeting. At the end of 1952, Party leaders decided to embark upon a program of rapid industrialization based on the Soviet model. By 1956 "the private sector of the urban economy had ceased to exist, and all industrial and commercial enterprises of any significant size had effectively been nationalized."[29] In the countryside, too, "collective ownership" was instituted and farming coopera-tives/collectives were formed with the aim of improving agricul-tural productivity for urban industrialization.[30] In recent decades, a widespread consensus has emerged that this turn to Sovietization was not only ill advised and ultra-leftist, but also anti-Marxist insofar as it effectively rejected the progressive and necessary role that markets and even capitalism must play in developing "advanced productive forces." This sentiment informed the official rationales of the Deng regime when it origi-nally embarked on market reforms, was embraced by Chinese liberals eager to repudiate the Maoist legacy, and has even been picked up by left scholars (like Lippit and Meisner).[31] There is an element of truth to this characterization, insofar as the CCP's decision was likely guided by a genuine desire to hasten the arrival of socialism. But as Meisner himself notes, the decision was also prompted by geopolitical concerns over national security in the wake of the Korean War and American military encirclement, as well as long-term nationalist goals of restoring China's status as a "wealthy and powerful" country.[32] Despite the hallowed tenets of orthodox Marxist stage theory, New

Democratic capitalism only seemed destined to achieve industrialization at a snail's pace, if at all; the Soviet model, on the other hand, offered a ready-made blueprint.

The planned economy that resulted from the "socialization" campaign of the mid-1950s was qualitatively similar to that which existed in the Soviet Union and Eastern Europe, but also possessed its own peculiarities. Both the family labor and capitalist sectors of pre-revolutionary China were virtually eliminated, and market exchange severely restricted.[33] Ho-fung Hung describes the "national regime of accumulation" under Mao as grounded on centralized state coordination of all economic resources, enabling the extraction of agrarian surplus through the "price scissors" between agricultural and industrial products.[34] With agricultural collectivization, the entire rural population became members of collective production brigades, while most of the urban population became members of work units organized at state-owned and collective enterprises, government offices, and institutions. Although workers were paid a wage, labor power was not a commodity. Rural production brigades and urban work units could not fire their members, and were responsible for organizing production and providing members' consumption.[35] The party-state provided free health care, education, and other social services through these urban and rural units, allowing for a rapid improvement in basic living standards.

Although it is common today for mainstream commentators to portray the Mao period as one of unmitigated backwardness and stagnation, the reality is quite different.[36] Between 1952 and the close of the Mao era, industrial output increased at an average per annum rate of 11.2 percent, and even maintained an average of 10 percent during the tumultuous decade of the Cultural Revolution.[37] As Meisner suggests, "the Mao period was one of the great modernizing epochs of world history, comparable to the most intensive periods in the industrialization of Germany,

Japan, and Russia—the other major latecomers to the modern industrial scene."[38] Income growth was relatively small throughout the period, especially for peasants, resulting in growing inequality between urban and rural areas. However, such measures do not take into account greater public consumption (education, health care, and welfare provisions for the elderly and destitute), which enabled dramatic improvements in key social and demographic indicators like literacy, life expectancy, nutrition and sanitation. When these factors are included, China compared favourably with countries possessing five times its per capita GNP.[39]

Still, the economic contradictions that accumulated by the close of the Mao era were profound. Agricultural output grew slightly more rapidly than population, but this was achieved only through the expansion of the agricultural labor force by 100 million. Labor productivity in agriculture is estimated to have *declined* by 15 percent during the Mao era.[40] The surplus available for urban investment was therefore increasingly thin, and threatened to disappear altogether. Nor was the loss of agricultural surplus being recouped through greater industrial labor productivity. After rising by over 50 percent during the First Five-Year Plan (1953-57), it then stagnated, increasing by only 2.1 percent per annum over the last two decades of the Mao era.[41] In short, the problems of the Maoist economy resembled those of all Stalinist-type "command economies": high industrial growth rates could only be accomplished with ever-higher capital investment, which in turn required an expanding accumulation rate (the proportion of national product withheld from consumption for investment).[42] According to Meisner, "As the consumption and popular living standards suffered, the accumulation rate rose to maintain the high pace of heavy industrial development. Without real gains in productivity, it is unlikely that these high levels of accumulation and investment could have been sustained much longer without impoverishing the population."[43] Mao's China, like Stalin's Russia, excelled in "extensive growth" by adding ever more workers and factories; but it too faced a crisis if it could not switch to "intensive growth," the systematic adoption of productivity-increasing methods and technologies by productive units (i.e., Smithian growth).[44]

An understanding of how and why Mao's China reached this impasse is crucial for understanding the post-Mao reform period. Yet the analyses of *China and Socialism* and *Adam Smith in Beijing* fall short in this respect. Arrighi has little to say about the dynamics of the Maoist command economy, emphasizing only that they provided a solid and egalitarian social substrate for the reintroduction of the market. His casual characterization of Mao's China as "socialist" must also be rejected, given its very real divergence from the society of abundance that Marx envisaged. Hart-Landsberg and Burkett are much more sophisticated, recognizing the mounting contradictions identified by Meisner and maintaining that China, at the time of Mao's death in 1976, "remained far from achieving the promises of socialism."[45] They rightly note the inability of workers and peasants to "exercis[e] democratic control over their economic and political life."[46] But they are somewhat unclear on precisely *why and in what way* this lack of worker's democracy contributed to the problems of Maoist China and what deficiencies its implementation would correct. They suggest that the needed form of restructuring was "decentralization of the economy and state decision-making" to enable direct control by the associated producers over the conditions and products of their labor.[47] This is of a piece with their overall vision of socialism, which would entail "autocentric integration of domestic needs, domestic demand, and domestic resource use."[48]

There are a number of problems with this thesis. First, it ignores the extent to which technological backwardness placed severe limits on China's "autocentric" developmental efforts, valorizing the national while implicitly rejecting Marx's dictum that socialism can only be achieved on the basis of highly advanced productive forces and the international division of labor. Emphasizing the productive forces does not mean retreating to a Dengist strategy of fostering market competition (as Hart-Landberg and Burkett fear); instead, it highlights the necessity of international socialist coordination and planning, rather than the autarky of socialism in one country. Second, Hart-Landsberg and Burkett assume that decentralizaton and more autonomous local decision-making is required for greater democracy. However, this is not so, and seems to take for granted that centralized planning cannot also be democratic. As was highlighted in the discussion of socialist planning above, workplace democracy must be integrated with macro-level planning undertaken by democratically-elected congresses at the national and international levels. While decentralization of certain tasks and decisions may be advantageous, it can also be highly deleterious to adequate planning. Maoist China was itself one of the most decentralized of the command economies. At the height of central planning, no more than 600 commodities had their price fixed by Beijing, only a hundredth of the number fixed by Moscow.[49] In *both* Maoist and post-Maoist China, decentralized industrialization strategies, although undertaken with different motivations, have led to the costly reproduction of unnecessary, small-scale plant.[50] Greater local democracy might help to ameliorate some of these difficulties, but it cannot surmount them.

The political economy of bureaucratic collectivism

To fully understand the developmental contradictions of Maoist China, we must achieve a more systemic appreciation of the class dynamics at work in the Soviet-type command economies. This is hardly an easy or uncontroversial task. But increasing temporal distance from the twentieth century does not absolve Marxists of an obligation to understand these societies. Strikingly, the theory that has gained most traction among historical materialists in the post-Soviet period is also the most inadequate: "state capitalism." Mike Haynes, Paresh Chattopadhyay, Neil Fernandez, Stephen Resnick and Richard Wolff have all penned major works in the last two decades describing the Soviet Union as some form of state-controlled capitalism.[51] The tremendous variety within this broad school is facilitated by a shared inability to recognize the *sine qua non* of capitalism, *viz.* market dependent reproduction of appropriators and producers alike. The incoherence of this approach is well illustrated by the taxonomical pirouettes its advocates have been forced to take when describing China. In a couple of recent works, for example, Alex Callinicos has maintained his long-held position that Mao's China was a "bureaucratic state capitalism"; that the implementation of Deng's reforms effected a transition "from one form of capitalism to another";[52] that this *new* form of capitalism has nevertheless enacted "a particularly concentrated and harsh version of what Marx called primitive accumulation of capital in which hundreds of millions of people, along with productive resources previously in the public domain, have been subordinated to the logic of global competition";[53] and finally, that this new form of capitalism has held up particularly well in the recent global crisis because it is…"state-capitalist"![54] The need for concepts that can identify the specificities of non-capitalist, yet non-socialist, societies should be apparent.

Aside from "state capitalism," two other major Marxist traditions have been offered for understanding the Soviet Union and other command economies: the degenerated/deformed workers' state thesis and variants of "bureaucratic collectivism." As Martin Thomas has argued, the distinctions between the three traditions have not always been hard and fast, contributing to a great degree of conceptual fuzziness and confusion.[55] For our purposes, though, the beginning of wisdom is to recognize that class relations of Soviet-type societies were not capitalist class relations. So what type of class societies were they?[56]

Historically, the thesis of bureaucratic collectivism gained recognition and traction as a critical response to Trotsky's analysis of the Stalinist Soviet Union as a degenerated workers' state. Trotsky's theory was subsequently elaborated and extended by various authors in the post-war period to describe newly established Soviet-type societies in Eastern Europe, China and beyond, societies which were then termed "deformed workers' states."[57] Defenders of this position recognize the non-socialist character of the command economies, but argue that they were still transitional workers' states. The major obstacle to socialist development, however, is the ruling nationalist party-state bureaucracy which actively suppressed workers' democracy domestically and rejected the necessity of workers' rule abroad, the two essential conditions for developing the productive forces in a socialist direction. At the same time, the ruling bureaucracy was conceived as a contradictory caste, rather than a new ruling class, because the basis of its privileges were the collectivized property forms typical of a workers' state. Trotsky outlined the argument thus:

> A class is defined not by its participation in the distribution of the national income alone, but by its independent role in the general structure of the economy and by its independent roots in the economic foundation of society. Each class (the feudal nobility, the peasantry, the petty bourgeoisie, the capitalist bourgeoisie and the proletariat) works out its own special forms of property. The bureaucracy lacks all these social traits. It has no independent position in the process of production and distribution. It has no independent property roots. Its functions relate basically to the political *technique* of class rule....

To put it plainly, insofar as the bureaucracy robs the people (and this is done in various ways by every bureaucracy) we have to deal not with *class exploitation*, in the scientific sense, but with *social parasitism*, although on a very large scale.[58]

Meisner has made broadly similar observations with respect to China, concluding that the Maoist bureaucracy "lacked several of the essential social and material attributes of a class."[59] As a caste rather than a class, Trotsky observed that the bureaucracy displayed "all shades of political thought... from genuine Bolshevism... to outright fascism."[60] Given this bifurcation between collectivized property forms and parasitic bureaucracy, the task of socialists is identified as defending the existing state (and nationalized property) from the threat of internally or externally induced counter-revolution, while also urging a *political* revolution to oust the bureaucracy and open the road to genuine socialist development.

The deformed workers' state analysis possesses genuine strengths, especially as a compass for political intervention. It recognizes that collectivized property and centralized planning, even if organized by a repressive and brutal bureaucracy, represents a real social gain for workers, and hints at what may be possible under genuine workers' rule. (The tremendous social advances in Maoist China are a testament to this.) It also illuminates the potentially brittle and contradictory nature of the bureaucracy as an ostensibly socialist stratum. Insofar as the bureaucracy justifies its existence and political rule on the basis of socialist ideals and Marxism in particular, it is also subject to contestation and challenge on the basis of those same ideals. The very ideological foundation of its legitimacy, in other words, is also inherently self-undermining. This points, in medium- and long-term perspectives at least, to two possible routes out of the half-way house of bureaucratic commandism: either workers' political rule or the establishment of a different, non-socialist ideological basis for the legitimacy and privileges of the ruling stratum.

Still, the deformed workers' state thesis also suffers from severe limitations, not least in its conception of class and exploitation. Trotsky and his followers used a classical Marxist theory of historical development to maintain that each class society developed on the basis of specific forms of property in the means of production and attendant relations of production. Since the bureaucracy rules on the basis of collectivized property forms typical of a workers' state, it is held to effect merely distributive rather than productive relations, and therefore cannot be a distinct, exploitative class. As we saw above, however, it was not forms of property in the means of production itself that distinguished different class societies (since this was almost always land) but rather the specific ways in which surplus is appropriated from direct producers. This observation, in turn, merits an expansion of our understanding of "forms of property." In feudalism, for example, it was property in the means of violence that ensured access to socially produced surplus, while in absolutist societies it was property in the state (office).[61] Indeed, Trotsky himself captures this distinction (without drawing out its implications) when he noted that in the Soviet Union, "The means of production belong to the state. But the state, so to speak, 'belongs' to the bureaucracy."[62]

With these historical parallels in mind, Brenner developed a particular variant of bureaucratic-collectivist analysis by arguing that, in important respects, the Soviet Union resembled pre-capitalist societies—even a "quasi-feudal society."[63] The bureaucracy constituted a ruling class that strove to maximize the total social surplus because "the greater the social surplus available to it, the more easily it can achieve any particular aim(s) it may have."[64] Since workers possess employment guarantees and are thus effectively merged with their means of production and subsistence, the bureaucracy has little to gain by forcing unemployment, and its managerial control is consequently limited. Accumulation and reinvestment is compelled, among other things, by geopolitical factors; yet, without either workers' democracy or the imperatives of market-dependent reproduction, there is no systematic drive to stimulate and innovate. After extensive growth has been exhausted, therefore, the bureaucracy is forced to simply squeeze ever more surplus from the workers, or "attempt to get the advantages of a market society within that set of non-capitalist property relations." The failure of market reforms, in turn, starkly poses two alternatives: capitalism or democratic socialism.[65]

Brenner's interpretation of bureaucratic collectivism identifies many of the same dynamics and contradictions as the deformed workers' state thesis, but does so in terms that are more consistent with the political Marxist understanding of capitalism's specificity. When considered in light of Trotsky's own concept of combined and uneven development, Brenner's analysis helps to contextualize and clarify Trotsky's thesis of the caste. The brittle, contradictory, and heterogeneous characteristics of the bureaucracy are not *sociological* hallmarks of its "non-class" character, but *historical* ramifications of its emergence as a novel, non-capitalist ruling class *within* a world already shaped by capitalist statehood and a capitalist world market. Having repressed the possibility of workers' democracy and prioritized the achievement of national power above international socialist solidarity, this class was rather quickly confronted with the fact that the non-capitalist social property relations that provided the basis for its privileges were ultimately incommensurate with the maintenance of those privileges, given geopolitical pressures emanating from more productive capitalist powers. The example of advanced capitalism also provided a check on the bureaucracy's ability to exert coercion, as too much might compel workers and intellectuals to view capitalism as a favourable alternative (as eventually happened in the Eastern Bloc). The broad spectrum of ideological and policy responses by various Soviet-type bureaucracies across time and space—ranging from neo-Stalinist authoritarianism to wholesale capitalist restoration—are thus born from a common dilemma. In this context, the attractions of market socialism, and its widespread adoption by command economies at various points, is readily apparent: it seems the surest way of improving productivity without sacrificing overall bureaucratic control of the surplus or introducing workers' democracy. [66]

The weakness of Brenner's bureaucratic collectivism is its lack of attention to the political questions that so animated Trotsky.[67] Brenner, like previous theorists of bureaucratic collectivism, was primarily concerned with highlighting the *reactionary* nature of the Soviet Union.[68] When compared with a regime of workers' democracy, this assessment is clearly correct; it is much more questionable when compared against the capitalist alternative, especially as it has been experienced in most of the Third World. Does collectivized property and the merger of direct producers represent a social gain to be defended against the prospect of privatization and capitalist restoration (as Trotsky suggested)? Or is it of little consequence for direct producers, given bureaucratic class rule through property in the state? The latter answer may have seemed reasonable at the time of Brenner's writing, when few workers were rising to challenge the dismantling of the command economies and state property. In light of the subsequent social catastrophe visited on the ex-USSR in particular, and the contours of China's own workers' struggles, Trotsky's answer appears much stronger.

It is worth noting, in this connection, a significant difference between the Soviet-type societies and absolutism. In both, the ruling class secured access to surplus through "property" in the state; however, the nature of this property, and the terms on which access was secured, were very different. In absolutist societies the fusion of the public and private was instituted through proprietary kingship, in which the monarch held the state as personal property. French monarch Louis XIV's infamous proclamation, *"l'état, c'est moi"* ["I am the state"] was far more than a rhetorical flourish—it was a reproductive principle of absolutist sovereignty. The monarch's granting of offices, increasingly by cash sale, represented an alienation of state power to private persons, who held them as proprietary, irrevocable, and hereditary.[69] Notions of divine law provided ideological justification and support for the system.[70] In Soviet-type societies, however, the state is not the personal property of a monarch, but the political property of Communist Parties. Government office and positions of enterprise management are not alienated as proprietary and hereditary, but allocated by the Party according to various criteria of assessment, especially the fulfilment of output targets and guaranteeing social stability.

The legitimacy of the Party's claim on the state, meanwhile, rests upon formal socialist and Marxist ideology, and the commitment to egalitarianism, workers' rule, and popular participation that such an ideology implies.[71] The import of these principles also goes beyond the merely ideological. In various forms they are also enshrined in law, from the declarations of the national constitution to the guidelines of enterprise management. To say that they are honoured mainly in the breach should be obvious. Yet, as broad components of the political apparatus, they nevertheless constitute a material factor in the bureaucracy's claim to politically-constituted property, and therefore its very reproduction as a ruling class. As a result, it also has profound potential to shape the contours of both inter- and intra-ruling class struggle. Most significantly, the direct producers (workers and peasants) can mobilize socialist ideals to stake a claim to genuine workers' rule and corollary institutions of workers' democracy, challenging the very existence of the bureaucracy itself and possibly causing it to fracture. This was the aim of Trotsky's political revolution. In the context of market reforms and the dispossession of direct producers, however, we can also envision less dramatic and polarizing forms of struggle which nevertheless are highly important in shaping the course of political economic change. The socialist trappings of the law and ideology may be used by workers and peasants to challenge the validity of market reforms and preserve their non-market access to the means of production. Such struggles would be conducted *against* sections of the bureaucracy and intelligentsia seeking to expand the ambit of market relations; but they may also dovetail with the short term interests of sections of the bureaucracy that seek to counter or reverse marketization measures threatening their own access to surplus. In this light, there is often a dynamic political economic process underlying Chinese attempts to secure what they euphemistically term "social stability," in which a variety of class actors seek to defend, challenge and transform prevailing social property relations.

To summarize the argument of this section, China was never a socialist society (contra Arrighi), nor was its economic difficulties in the late 1970s significantly induced by over-centralization (contra Hart-Landsberg and Burkett). The lack of workers' democracy in China was and is crippling, but it must be positioned within a more systemic understanding of the class dynamics at work in Soviet-type economies, and the contradictions these dynamics imparted both internally (in processes of surplus extraction) and externally (in processes of geopolitical and nationalist competition). The confluence of internal and external challenges called into question the ability of the bureaucracy to reproduce itself using existing methods. During intraparty debates a decade after reform began, Deng maintained: "there was no way the economy could develop, no way living standards could rise, and no way the country could get stronger... The world is galloping forward these days, a mile a minute, especially in science and technology. We can hardly keep up."[72]

Yet neither a turn to capitalism nor the implementation of workers' democracy could be achieved without dismantling the politically-constituted property providing the basis for bureaucratic privilege. The introduction of market relations within the existing system of bureaucratic collectivism therefore appeared to be a silver bullet against stagnation and collapse, allowing the maintenance of state ownership while achieving efficiencies guaranteed by the market.[73] Deng was not being facetious when he maintained in 1989 that "Some people, of course, understand 'reform' to mean movement towards liberalism or capitalism. Capitalism is the heart of reform for them, but not for us."[74] Like Adam Smith, Arrighi, and various market socialists, the Beijing bureaucrats assumed that the efficiency-enhancing behaviours of profit-maximization, cost-cutting and innovation could be secured simply by expanding opportunities for commodity production and allowing market competition to work its magic— without, at the same time, imperilling state ownership or the broader plan.[75] However, such efficiency-driven behaviour constitutes the very "laws of motion" of capitalism itself, and is only impelled when producers and appropriators lose non-market access to their means of subsistence, transforming the market from opportunity to imperative. Determining the extent to which this has been achieved in contemporary China is therefore the key to assessing the validity of Hart-Landsberg and Burkett's "capitalist restoration" and the enduring significance of Arrighi's "accumulation by dispossession."

Chapter Five

Deng Xiaoping's Market Turn

In 1978, under Deng's newly-consolidated leadership, the CCP assessed the declining performance of the planned economy under Mao. Drawing upon the Marxist historical stage theory and "objective economic laws" that were once so prominent in guiding the Party's practice, the CCP revived the original logic of New Democracy. Echoing the Mao of 1949, the Party now declared that it was the "remnants of feudalism" that posed the true barrier to modern economic development, and that "the only socialism we can imagine is one based on all the lessons learnt though large-scale capitalist culture."[1] To overcome the impasse it was thought necessary to introduce a "planned commodity economy," maintaining state ownership but introducing the efficiencies of production for sale on the market.[2]

In the thirty years that followed, China became, in the words of one economist, "a world-record holder" in GDP growth. Official statistics record an annual pace of 9.9 percent growth between 1978 and 2007; even the most sceptical analysts suggest a figure of no lower than 9 percent for the same period.[3] This rate was maintained at the height of the global recession in 2009 and 2010, and declined only slightly in 2012 and 2013 (to 7.8 percent).[4] For liberal economists and financial journalists, there is little that needs to be explained in these numbers. China's astonishing growth in the reform period is a simple tale of smashing barriers to trade, eliminating restrictions on profit-making, and generally unleashing the Smithian "animal spirits of the ordinary Chinese, many of whom have grabbed the chance to make money for the first time in decades."[5] So repressed were these spirits during thirty years of Maoism that they did not even need the usual foundation of secure private property rights in order to soar. Tom Bethell, for example, devotes an entire book to establishing the hallowed liberal principle "that the widespread and secure ownership of property is the *sine qua non* of prosperity."[6] Yet in Dengist China, he finds that "the absence of the rule of law seemed to be no obstacle to what may have been the most rapid economic advance ever. There was no need for an understanding of the common law, or Roman law—of any particular system of law."[7] Market forces seemed to work their magic regardless of formal ownership—precisely what Deng had suggested!

Marxists have been much more attentive to the shifting and conflict-ridden social relations underlying the Chinese growth "miracle." As with Hart-Landsberg and Burkett, however, an abstract model of capitalism is often utilized to explain why markets themselves have certain social effects. Market reforms "have a dynamic of their own," and once marketization had been decided upon, "market imperatives quickly proved uncontrollable."[8] Although they are often very skilful at revealing the contradictory process of market reform, like their liberal nemeses they do not adequately identify the specificity of capitalist markets, taking for granted that markets contain the seeds of capitalism. What must be uncovered is the process by which, and *the extent* to which, market dependence has been instantiated through a qualitative transformation of China's social property relations.

Agrarian reform: Markets without capitalism in the countryside

What is remarkable, in this context, is the extent to which bureaucratic collectivism remained in place, even into the early 1990s, *despite* marketization.[9] Neither in agriculture nor in state enterprises was there a qualitative transformation of the bureaucratic economy towards market-driven, productivity-maximizing growth. This counters the analysis offered by many liberal scholars and journalists, who have come to see the rural reforms, in particular, as the first liberating step towards capitalism. Richard McGregor, for example, suggests that "every farming household... turned themselves into mini-businesses,"[10] while Yasheng Huang regards the period as a golden era of "entrepreneurial" (rather than "state-led") capitalism.[11] Both writers interpret the "collectively owned" status of township and village enterprises (TVEs) as little more than a legal fiction.[12] While coming from a different normative standpoint, prominent critical scholars have also echoed this view. Hart-Landsberg and Burkett effectively equate de-collectivization with *privatization*, suggesting that land became "the private property of those families that had contracted for its use," and that "those in possession of contracted land had full rights to rent it, sell it, or pass it on to their heirs."[13] TVEs, in turn, are characterized as "private enterprises in disguise."[14] For his part, Minqi Li suggests that agriculture was "in effect privatized" through the new "household responsibility system."[15]

Such conclusions are understandable given the dramatic restructuring that took place within state enterprises and its consequences for the urban proletariat. Yet even today, after tens of millions have left the farms in search of urban jobs, 40 percent of China's labor force still subsists in agriculture.[16] Because rural areas have provided the major source of new urban proletarians, it is all the more necessary to develop a nuanced and accurate understanding of agricultural social relations. The abolition of the commune system certainly precipitated dramatic decay in rural infrastructure and social support systems. However, Arrighi, Amin, and others are quite correct to point out that land is far from being privatized, either in law or in fact. The dismantling of the agricultural production teams revived independent household production while also creating a novel form of land management. The village collectives established a right to the use and supervision of land but no right to buy or sell.[17] Land use rights were allocated to peasant households through a two-field system, with some plots being distributed on a per capita basis (and therefore subject to redistribution with demographic change), while most (termed "responsibility land") were distributed on 15-year contracts, subject to a government grain procurement quota. This responsibility land, moreover, also tended to be contracted on a per capita basis (rather than concentrated in the hands of a small number of "entrepreneurial" farmers), and assigned in multiple, separate plots to ensure equality of soil type.[18] All essential elements of this system remain in place today, although procurement quotas have generally been replaced with direct price subsidies.[19]

Clarifying the nature of land access and use rights in China is essential for understanding the particular way in which market relations entered the countryside. The language of "privatization" is often used by critical scholars to suggest that what is privatized (i.e., the means of production) becomes capital, leading to concentration of ownership and accumulation. What is decisive, however, is whether access to the means of production is *dependent* upon successful commodity production. Private ownership of land does not automatically turn producers into capitalists; likewise, state ownership of the land can greatly facilitate capitalist production if leases are determined on a competitive basis (something that is happening in urban China).[20] The household responsibility system, however, not only maintained direct, non-market access to the means of production for peasant households; it also did so through a highly egalitarian mechanism of land use distribution and redistribution. As a result, Chris Bramall notes, "the market for land in rural China is far removed from that found in most other countries, whether developed or under-developed."[21]

Polarization in the countryside has not come about through dispossession, but instead through differential responses to market opportunities.[22] Without the imperative to reinvest their surpluses in agricultural production, many peasants in the early reform period invested in sideline industries, especially after the government lowered its grain procurement price in the mid-1980s.[23] Philip Huang observed:

> To put it bluntly, marketized farming in the 1980s did no better in crop production than it did in the six centuries between 1350 and 1950, or than collective agriculture did in the previous three decades.
>
> The crucial development in the [Yangtze] delta... came not from the "private" crop production and petty commerce that were given so much press but rather from rural industry and new sidelines.[24]

One important new source of income was remittances. Members of agricultural households with surplus labor began to migrate to urban areas in search of wage employment, including in the newly established Special Economic Zones (SEZs) of Guangdong and Fujian. This constituted the first wave of tens of millions of migrants who moved to the coastal cities to provide sweatshop labor for foreign investors and, increasingly, domestic Chinese capitalists. For these migrants, the household registration system (*hukou*) that guarantees their family access to agricultural land also denies them residency status and attendant benefits in the cities, leaving them vulnerable to harsh super-exploitation.[25] The extra income remitted to their families was and continues to be significant. Only by understanding agricultural land use as a subsistence right, rather than as capital, can we make sense of the curious fact that the *poorest* families in rural China tend to have the most land. The incomes of (relatively) richer households are usually boosted by the additional sources of income outlined above.[26]

The absence of market dependence among agricultural

producers did not, however, ensure prosperity. At best, it delivered modestly improving living standards when the government increased procurement prices or subsidies and invested in improved technological inputs; at worst, it has continued the pattern of involutionary, labor-intensive growth that does not lighten the load on the direct producer.[27] Yet it is also "a crucial resource that is denied to farmers in most other countries," and is appreciated as such by most peasants.[28] The struggle to maintain non-market access to the means of subsistence and to prevent capitalization is of crucial importance in contemporary conflicts over land expropriation and dispossession. Indeed, it would be very difficult to understand the significance of current peasant struggles, which are often directed against illegal appropriation of land use rights by township governments, if we accepted that the peasantry were *already* dispossessed and market-dependent.

Rise and fall of the TVEs

For over a decade, the main absorber of rural surplus labor was not the SEZs but the TVEs. Contrary to much received wisdom, the TVEs were not, in the main, private enterprises.[29] Many of those established near the coastal SEZs were funded by investors from Hong Kong and Taiwan, and their official status as "collective" was indeed a convenient and necessary fiction, referred to as donning the "red hat."[30] Throughout the rest of the country, though, most TVEs were established by local governments to recover revenues lost as a result of the 1983 fiscal reform, which officially required that "each level of government has its own budget."[31] As politically-constituted enterprises whose production and sales occurred outside central planning, the TVEs perfectly expressed the inherent contradictions of market socialism. On the one hand, as Arrighi notes, the township authorities sought to utilize their revenue streams for political ends. Mandates required that enterprise profits be used to augment welfare and bonus funds, construct local infrastructure (including water supply to households, improved schools and roads); improve public social services; subsidize farm incomes; and maximize employment by taking on redundant labor.[32] On the other hand, such non-economic obligations placed the TVEs at a competitive disadvantage against capitalist firms (which faced no such restraints) and local governments lacked the policy capacity and resources to shelter TVEs from competition over the long term. The result was ballooning debt levels as township governments devised a variety of funding vehicles to sustain the TVE taxes and profits that constituted the bulk of revenues.[33] The sustainability of the TVEs was certainly imperilled by their production for increasingly competitive markets. However, the firms were only made market-dependent by political decisions in the late 1990s: primarily the tightening of loan provisions by the central government, and secondarily the large-scale privatization of SOEs (with which many TVEs had contracts).[34] As a result of these decisions, "many township enterprises simply collapsed overnight, and only a handful that were in better shape were transformed into private enterprises."[35]

Critics of market socialism are quite correct to emphasize the sobering aspects of the TVE narrative. In his enthusiasm for market competition, Arrighi, for one, seems to completely miss the fact that at the time of his writing, collective firms represented only 10 percent of total TVE employment.[36] Yet, when considered from the perspective of specifically capitalist rules of reproduction, what stands out even in the TVE experience is the politically mediated way that relations of full market dependence were instituted. Although the enterprises were produced outside the plan and were of relatively recent vintage, bankruptcy had to be forced on them (and therewith, many local governments) by destroying the political mechanisms that ensured their maintenance. Effectively separated from their politically-constituted enterprises, township officials became increasingly reliant on alternative means for ensuring their reproduction—means that had already made an appearance among local governments throughout the country after the 1984 and 1994 fiscal reforms. The latter established the so-called "cadre responsibility system" by which local officials sign performance contracts pledging to attain certain targets imposed by higher-level governments. The criteria of these contracts include development targets, remittance of tax and profits, and maintenance of social order.[37] Before the tightening of financial screws in the late 1990s, TVEs were considered an ideal vehicle for meeting all criteria. Their loss dictated that township governments alter their form of "local state corporatism" to one reliant upon the competitive performance of private enterprises and privatized TVEs (as well as those TVEs that remained profitable).[38]

Successful "developmental" townships thus came to resemble miniature versions of capitalist developmental states, in which fiscal and therefore political results are structurally dependent upon crafting an effective regulatory environment for the reproduction of market-dependent enterprises.[39] The tax resources for meeting social and political goals (and thereby social stability) may expand in the process, but profits are no longer directly extracted and controlled by township governments through ownership claims on enterprises. Satisfying requirements of social stability became dependent, in turn, on the vagaries of market accumulation. Those township governments that could rely less upon taxation of competitive enterprises employed political office and coercion for "predatory" ends: the levying of arbitrary fines, exactions and payments to satisfy the criteria of performance contracts. Although such "off-budgetary funds" were often collected from enterprises,[40] it was the peasant population—with its guaranteed access to land—that provided the most stable and reliable source of surplus exaction. After the collapse and privatization of the TVEs, peasants came to carry a taxation burden four times larger than that of urban residents, despite urban incomes being several times larger.[41] Such exactions boosted local township government revenues while threatening to provoke peasant resistance and the goal of social stability.[42] In this way, the abstract assessment criteria of the cadre responsibility system, while designed to achieve harmonious, market-driven local growth, actually yielded a diversity of political economic regimes and forms of social conflict. The bankruptcy and privatization of TVEs hastened the establishment of capitalist social property relations in many locales, while reinforcing politically-mediated extraction of peasant surplus in others.

Deng's SOE reforms: Profiteering without intensive growth

If instituting market-driven reproduction was fraught with difficulty even in the townships, it was all the more so at higher levels of government and in urban areas where three decades of state industrial development had powerfully shaped the non-capitalist reproductive strategies of the working class, SOE managers, and government officials. In the grand vision of the reformers, market efficiencies were to be secured in a three-step process of deepening reform: first, the devolution of authority to enterprise managers and the introduction of state/enterprise profit-sharing; second, the freeing of prices to enable cost-cutting responses to market demand; and third, the threat of bankruptcy and unemployment ("hard budget constraints").[43] Yet the basis of bureaucratic-collectivist social property relations lay in the Party's direct control of the economy and surpluses, organized through the plan and implemented by SOEs. Maintaining the plan and the efficacy of state enterprises, in turn, required extensive forms of intervention that militated *against* market-dependent reproduction: rationing inputs of labor, raw materials, and means of production; determining what products and how much output could be sold on the market; arbitrary taxation of profitable firms and redistribution of surplus to those unprofitable; disallowing lay-offs of redundant or inefficient labor; and refusing to allow market forces to force bankruptcy upon enterprises.[44] Writing in 1994, Richard Smith cogently captured the contradictions of the "planned commodity economy" in a way that evoked the familiar dilemma of market socialism:

> [O]n the one hand, to the extent that [the bureaucracy] preserved the bulk of the state-owned, state-planned economy intact, they could only do so by intervening in ways that subverted their own project of 'commiditizing' the planned economy. On the other hand, to the extent that they actually allowed market forces to restructure production, to re-allocate resources, to redistribute incomes—which they did, but only on the margins of the bureaucratic-state economy—they eventually permitted the growth of a sizeable private and semi-private capitalist economy *outside the state economy*.[45]

Reforms such as profit-sharing *did* alter the incentives of enterprise managers and even made them more market-oriented; but without the real threat of bankruptcy they were not made into capitalists. Instead, retained earnings and other claims to revenue were utilized to maximize extensive investment and consumption (the "two expansions"), rather than productivity-enhancing investment and cost-cutting.[46] Indeed, Dic Lo refers to a "consumption revolution" during this early phase of reform,[47] which has also been described as "reform without losers."[48] Wages continued to be distributed on an egalitarian basis, rather than according to performance; "market blockades" were erected by local governments to protect their SOEs; local officials built "huge numbers of small-scale uneconomic factories of every description, leading to widespread duplication of plant"; and the dual-price structure of plan and market enabled profiteering through arbitrage rather than competitive production.[49]

Intensive growth mainly occurred in the capitalist sector, both domestic Chinese-owned (still small by the early 1990s) and foreign-invested. Mao-era tendencies of declining productivity and quality control in state industry continued unabated, leaving the government increasingly reliant upon the capitalist sector to provide tax revenues and employment.[50] Extensive state industrial expansion in the early reform period was enabled by greater debt and direct foreign investment. By the early 1990s, however, export earnings were becoming an important source of revenue, offsetting reliance on foreign loans. When Deng made his famous "Southern Tour" of the Shenzhen SEZ in 1992 he sanctified the further development of the capitalist export sector, declaring that "as long as it makes money, it is good for China."[51] At its Fourteenth Party Congress in the same year the CCP declared its intention to establish a "socialist market economy with Chinese characteristics," seeming to resolve the stalemate between "conservatives" and reformers that had paralyzed the Party since the 1989 Tiananmen massacre.[52] For many critical political economists, this marked a decisive shift toward full capitalist restoration. The "socialist market economy," suggests Minqi Li, was in the Chinese context "a euphemism for capitalism."[53] With much greater nuance, Hart-Landsberg and Burkett note that "The significant development in this stage of the reform process was that the Party had now decided to abandon its long held commitment to state-owned enterprises as the central anchor of the Chinese economy."[54]

The post-1992 reforms, especially the privatization of state industry, were exceptionally important in shaping China's contemporary political economy. To contextualize their significance and extent, however, we have to understand why the previous decade of market reform failed to transform state industry. Why, in other words, did the bureaucratic class largely refuse to enforce bankruptcy and unemployment despite stated intentions to the contrary? To answer this question, it is necessary to identify the centrality of politically-constituted property forms in the reproductive strategies of both the ruling bureaucracy and the working class. Since the 1949 Revolution and especially the "socialization" campaign of the mid-1950s, state-owned property was integral to the reproduction of the bureaucracy. It afforded direct control over the economy and its surpluses, providing the basis for ruling class power and privilege. State enterprises also provided ideological legitimacy for the CCP's monopoly on power and its claim on politically-constituted property. The working class, for its part, did not accept the Party's rule without cynicism and contestation; yet its effective merger with the means of production also delivered real social benefits and guarded against the vagaries of unemployment and destitution. Widespread bankruptcy and lay-offs, therefore, not only raised the spectre of labor unrest—they also called into question the very *raison d'etre* of the Party itself. There were thus a number of considerations at play in intra-bureaucratic factional debates: how far the reforms could be pushed without imperilling the viability of state property; to what extent labor unrest would result; and to what degree such unrest, if sparked, would call into question the Party's political monopoly. Until the early 1990s, the Party's verdict was that reforms would have to fall well short of instituting market dependence among SOEs if the bureaucracy was to be maintained.

Examining the reform process from the standpoint of bureaucratic and working class relationships to state property raises important questions for analyzing capitalist restoration. Why did the bureaucracy opt for a course of instituting market dependence, and how far has it been taken? To what extent has struggle within the ruling class, and between the ruling class and direct producers, influenced or affected this course? Has the Party's socialist ideology and claim to legitimacy—the supposed "leading role" that the Communist Party assumes in taking the nation towards socialism—mattered at all? [55]

If the CCP's decision to abandon New Democracy was decisively conditioned by international developments and pressures, so too was the reformers' effort to transcend the half-way house of 1980s reforms. In December 1989, months after the events of Tiananmen, Deng and several Politburo members and senior cadres gathered to watch a videotape of events in Romania in which the family of Communist dictator Nicolae Ceauşescu was executed. For someone in the audience, the lesson was clear: "We'll be like this if we don't strengthen our proletarian dictatorship and repress the reactionaries." Deng replied, "Yes, we'll be like this if we don't carry out reforms and bring about benefits to the people."[56] Deng's argument won the day, and implied that the maintenance of Party rule, rather than depending upon a tightening of bureaucratic control over the economy, would require its weakening. Only the further expansion of market forces in all sectors of the economy could deliver "benefits to the people." In most journalistic and scholarly discourse on China, this shift is routinely interpreted as signalling a transformation in the Party's basis of legitimacy, from socialist ideals to "economic growth." There is a profound truth in this, illustrated by the glaring paradoxes and absurdities of the regime's official ideology. When Chen Yuan, a senior Party official and the son of China's pre-eminent economic planner, was needled about these contradictions by an American political scientist in the mid-1980s, he replied: "We are the Communist Party, and we will decide what communism is."[57] Yet, behind the Party's attempts to "decide" what communism is—and to reorient the social basis for economic growth—were real conflicts over the transformation of social property relations, conflicts that are not resolved even in the present.

Chapter Six

The Fifteenth Party Congress and the Era of Mass Privatization

Following Deng's "Southern Tour" certain limitations on the size of private enterprises and foreign investment were lifted. Increasingly, Party cadres began to "jump into the sea" of private enterprise, albeit with far greater connections inside the system to access contracts, licenses, credit and markets.[1] When combined with the small-scale household enterprises already in existence and the burgeoning TVEs, competition on product markets stiffened considerably. Despite shrinking relative importance in the national economy, both the output and employment of the state sector continued to grow in absolute terms even into the mid-1990s.[2] This familiar pattern of "double expansion" extensive growth was fuelled by mounting "non-performing loans" (NPLs) from state-owned banks. On average, the state-owned small and medium enterprises were losing money; SOE profits as a percentage of GDP plummeted from 14 percent in 1978 to almost zero in 1996.[3] Debt levels of Chinese enterprises soared to some of the highest in the world. The "soft budget constraint," therefore, continued to be the handmaiden of extensive growth divorced from concerns for productivity and cost-cutting.[4]

The Chinese leadership, then, faced a particularly acute form of the market socialist dilemma. SOEs, especially the large and medium enterprises still producing in the "downstream" sector, could no longer depend upon protected prices to generate surpluses. The only means of propping up such firms in the long run was to roll back the extent of market competition, which the leadership of President Jiang Zemin and Premier Zhu Rongji was quite unwilling to do. With such an option ruled out, the only other alternative, within the constraint of bureaucratic rule, was to actually enforce the verdict of the market: downsizing enterprises, allowing bankruptcies and ending guarantees to lifetime employment and other benefits.[5] The dramatic expansion of the domestic and foreign-invested capitalist sector, where workers enjoyed few if any of the benefits of their counterparts in the state sector, was invoked by the leadership to rationalize market dependence. State workers were portrayed as pampered, lazy and undeserving—not unlike the capitalist media portrayals of public workers in the advanced capitalist countries in recent years.[6] The expanding private sector, it was also suggested, would absorb those redundant state laborers that were cast adrift.

The way in which the endemic problems of the SOEs were to be overcome was expressed at the Fifteenth Party Congress in September 1997 as "grasping the large, and letting the small go."[7] In "grasping the large," the Party sought to focus its attention on the largest centrally controlled firms, reorganizing them into larger and more competitive enterprise groups and refinancing them on a renewed basis. In "letting the small go," local governments at various levels were given a green light to restructure, and especially to privatize and close down, those deemed unviable. Local governments were also pushed to do so, with concomitant reforms in the banking system encouraging a purge of NPLs from the balance sheets and a move from government-directed credit toward "commercial" lending principles.[8] Throughout this process, the external requirements and conditions of China's impending WTO membership was invoked by the Party leadership to press controversial and socially wrenching policies.[9]

Capitalist restoration from above?

In many respects, the decisions made at, and policies implemented after, the Fifteenth Party Congress appear to be a capitalist counter-revolution from above, marking the determination of the Chinese state class to finally transform its relationship with politically-constituted property. In massively privatizing state industry and altering the assessment criteria of state officials and managers to ensure market competitiveness in the state enterprises that remained, the state class seemed to repudiate its political claim to direct, non-market access to surplus. The original Dengist and market socialist vision of achieving market efficiency atop the existing system of state ownership and surplus command had finally run aground. Its contradictions could only be surmounted by crafting an authentically capitalist state, decisively separating the political from the economic. These policies also inaugurated a period of genuine primitive accumulation by Communist cadres who used legal and illegal means to obtain state assets.[10] The great majority of local state and collective enterprises were totally and partially privatized, with the initial system of distributing shares to all employees being supplanted with management buy-outs (MBOs). These "embourgeoisied cadres," moreover, seem to have systematically reinvested in production to a much greater extent than the Russian oligarchs—a curious phenomenon that has likely been facilitated by the maintenance of Communist political power, and the insider connections it affords to newly-christened cadre-capitalists.[11] In the process of state sector restructuring approximately 50 million workers, or 40 percent of the public sector workforce, were laid off. This was most certainly a phase of reform "with losers."[12]

While emphasizing different elements, most critical political economists and informed left-wing commentators seem to have reached a consensus that the reforms of the late 1990s definitively established the "capitalist restoration" identified by Hart-Landsberg and Burkett. A good case in point is Joel Andreas, who has written perhaps the most compelling Marxist rebuttal of Arrighi. He takes note of enduring state ownership in significant sectors and the use of public holding companies to pursue "state objectives that are broader than quarterly profits." Nevertheless, he argues that "the structure of these enterprises has been fundamentally changed so that they are required—and able—to make profitability their primary goal." Consequently, "almost all" enterprises, whether public or private, "now operate according to capitalist principles."[13] The government's strong support for the expansion of the capitalist sector, according to Andreas, confirms its character as a capitalist state. State officials "are expected to identify and support 'winners' in the economic competition. This expectation extends from the Political Bureau, which grooms national champions, down to county and township cadres, who are inveterate boosters of successful local enterprises."[14] Precisely because the huge state-owned enterprises in strategic sectors of the economy must focus on the bottom line, they appear much like the capitalist level in Braudel's hierarchy.[15]

The one exception to this thoroughgoing capitalization, according to Andreas, is agriculture—but even here commercial agriculture has made inroads with putting-out-style contracts and leasing of land. In October 2008 the CCP even announced its intention to allow the sale of land use rights to facilitate the concentration of land holdings.[16] In any case, "the land tenure system established in the 1980s has served the broader interests of capital," averting social instability while subsidizing the employers of migrant workers.[17] Although Andreas does not raise the point, it is worth noting that it was in fact Arrighi who originally made the claim that effective land possession by direct producers was often more functional for capital accumulation than outright dispossession and proletarianization.[18] This claim garnered Arrighi the "neo-Smithian" label, and is quietly reversed in his discussion of China in *Adam Smith in Beijing*.

Andreas' clever harnessing of Arrighi and Braudel to substantiate his claim that China is capitalist through and through should raise the eyebrows of historical materialists. There has undoubtedly been a dramatic fall in state employment, collapse of TVEs, crushing exploitation of migrant workers, class polarization, and sweeping loss of socialized goods and services. These sobering developments are all, in turn, very much connected to the development of capitalism in China and the generation of market-dependent social relations. Still, is it true that SOEs are now both "required" and "able" to make profits their primary goal? Are public and private enterprises equally run along "capitalist principles"? Have state officials at all levels of government really been reoriented towards "picking winners" in economic competition? What does it mean to say that land use rights have "served the broader interests of capital"? Would the expansion of commercial agriculture only serve the narrow interests of some capitalists? And if so, what does that say about the CCP today, seemingly on the precipice of promoting such agriculture? Is the Party thereby moving towards or away from capitalism? And where, for that matter, are peasants, workers, and intra-ruling-class political conflict in all of this?

Hart-Landsberg repeats some of Andreas' themes in his recent analysis of US-China relations in the midst of deep recession. Offering what he terms a "class-based analysis" of the global crisis, Hart-Landsberg endeavours to show that "it is capitalism—not competition between China and the United States—that is the source of [American workers'] economic problems." This cuts against the grain of much mainstream commentary as well as the demands of many trade unions in the US,[19] who suggest that "our task is to strengthen capitalist market forces in China."[20] These analyses, claims Hart-Landsberg, miss the fact that the Chinese government "has already transformed the country's economy along capitalist lines."[21] The leadership of the Communist Party has pushed the current growth strategy because it has been among its biggest beneficiaries, creating "a fusion of party-state-capitalist elites around a shared commitment to continue advancing capitalist restructuring." The children of Party officials ("princelings") are appointed to key positions in the state-owned enterprises, obtaining loans from government banks and enriching themselves with kickbacks. There are, to be sure, disputes over economic policy with the US—but these are merely "struggles over distributional issues."[22]

Hart-Landsberg's new analysis reproduces problems originally found in *China and Socialism* while extending them to the international plane. If China has "already transformed its economy along capitalist lines," what is left to be achieved by the "capitalist restructuring" that has yet to take place? One obvious factor might be reform of state enterprises and banks, but these now appear to have emerged as a tremendous source of capitalist profit-making alongside the foreign sector. It seems that we have no precise understanding of what is entailed by capitalist restructuring and how it is being contested. Without such an understanding it is difficult to fully accept Hart-Landsberg's claim that the "market forces" American commentators and policy-makers seek to extend are not in some way related to capitalism, i.e., the imperatives of market dependence. Indeed, Hart-Landsberg identifies US policy proposals, such as revaluing the Chinese currency, opening markets to US exports, and "play[ing] by the rules of competitive capitalism." What are the rules of capitalism, if not competitive?

Persistence of non-capitalist social property relations

Contra Andreas and Hart-Landsberg, the evolution of the Chinese political economy over the last decade and a half, in both domestic and international contexts, cannot be understood simply through the master categories of "capitalism" and "profits." Such categories are integral to the story, of course, as they have been for some time. However, the contradictions of what some have termed the "China model"[23] can only be understood by examining the continued importance of distinctly non-capitalist social property relations and ways of reproduction. The policies of Jiang and Zhu, while dramatically altering the weight and composition of the state sector, did not succeed in rendering what remained of the sector market dependent. The maintenance of politically-constituted enterprises reproduced not only the old patterns of extensive growth, but also militated against the construction of an authentically capitalist state form (that is, one based on the separation of the political and the economic). Understanding Chinese development in these terms also allows for an appreciation of the formative role of inter-and intra-class conflicts in shaping its evolution, and an illumination of the social substance underlying the Chinese side of global "imbalances." A central conclusion of this analysis is that the future of non-capitalist social relations remains an unresolved and highly contested element of Chinese politics.

As with so much of the reform process, the current conjuncture of Chinese political economy reflects the particular way in which market relations were imposed upon, and utilized by, economic actors in the state sector. Although some reporters dubbed the 1997 decision as "Big Bang Chinese-style" and most referred to it as "privatization," the Chinese leadership insisted on labelling it *Gaizhi*, or "transforming the system."[24] More than mere political correctness was at work here—the process resulted in an alphabet soup of hybrid ownership structures. Even those who have intensively studied Chinese statistics and records for years are not certain of the size of the private sector. Liberals such as Yasheng Huang bemoan that a pure private sector, without any government ties or involvement, contributes a "miniscule" 20 percent of industrial output.[25] In 2005, a Hong Kong brokerage firm released a celebratory report claiming that the private sector contributed 70 percent of GDP and employed 75 percent of the workforce. According to the report, the key economic question was not "How will the government respond to an economic slowdown?" but "How will Chinese entrepreneurs respond?"[26] A week later, the Swiss investment bank UBS issued a rejoinder, claiming that the private sector now accounted for more than 30 percent of the economy, "whichever indicator you used." According to the bank, in 2005 the state maintained 100 percent or majority ownership in oil, petrochemicals, mining, banks, insurance, telecoms, steel, aluminum, electricity, aviation, airports, railways, ports, highways, autos, health care, education and the civil service.[27]

Establishing precise figures of ownership type for the economy as a whole is therefore very difficult. What is much easier, and ultimately more important, is discerning sectoral trends. Even before the restructuring of the late 1990s, central government industry was increasingly concentrated in energy, natural resources, and other sectors of substantial economies of scale. Barriers to entry were either real or regulatory, and the enterprises remained largely profitable.[28] "Grasping the large" was thus a relatively straightforward matter of consolidating a few hundred, largely profitable SOEs in the "upstream" resource and capital-intensive industries.[29] Regulatory barriers to entry were maintained, while enterprise governance guidelines were altered to place greater emphasis on profitability, productivity and efficiency. A regime of "limited and managed competition" was introduced in most industries, such that two or more enterprises would always compete in the same product market.[30] The intention of this policy was to propel innovation, while preventing the sort of "over-competition" and depressed profit rates endemic to industrial capitalism.[31] "Corporatization," or the reorganization of SOEs into joint-stock companies, accelerated greatly after the late 1990s.[32] Minority shares in the reorganized enterprises were sold on domestic and foreign stock markets, with the intention of reinforcing market-based management. Stock market prospectuses, however, usually neglected to mention the central role of the Party committee in enterprise governance.[33]

Although these changes were significant, it would be misleading to suggest that they qualitatively transformed central enterprises into capitalist profit-maximizers. Lay-offs and reductions of employee benefits undoubtedly boosted profits, but were comparatively minor given the capital-intensive nature and monopoly positions of the industries. In the new decade, rising resource prices and a galloping domestic economy enabled them to grow much as they had previously: through continuous reinvestment of profits in extensive growth. The most important sectors under central government control by the late 2000s were petroleum and refining, metallurgy, electricity, military industry, and telecommunications.[34] According to Hart-Landsberg, in 2006 three state oil companies accounted for half the earnings of the 160 largest "state owned monopolies and oligopolies."[35] Between 2002 and 2012, revenues at two of China's largest SOEs—Sinopec (petroleum) and China Mobile (telecoms)—multiplied almost eight times, twice the rate of economic growth.[36]

The policy of fostering a small number of "national champions" that would be competitive in international product markets was much more ambitious, for it required a fundamental transformation in reproductive strategy. Rather than relying on government-backed monopoly or oligopoly positions in domestic markets, the success of these firms would depend on breaking into the oligopolistic *world* market through intensive growth and competitive innovations. In this, a handful of enterprises seem to have been at least partially successful, including Huawei (telecommunications equipment), Haier (consumer appliances), Lenovo (computers), and Baosteel (steel).[37] However, only the most "upstream" (Baosteel) is unambiguously state-controlled, while the most "downstream" (Huawei) is privately owned but politically well-connected. Haier, in fact, represents a fascinating case of a "red hat" urban collective in the city of Qingdao that actively frustrated attempts to place it under state control. In 2004 a Hong Kong academic, Larry Xianping, spurred a popular backlash against privatization when he exposed the ways MBOs had dispossessed workers. Haier, in particular, was fingered as a culprit in the effective theft of state assets.[38] The outcry became so loud, and echoed so highly in Party quarters, that Haier was declared a state enterprise by the Qingdao government in 2004 and MBOs were banned the next year. However, Haier's senior managers simply refused to attend meetings convened by the Qingdao state enterprise agency, and resisted orders to take over a failing state enterprise. Its obstinacy worked: in 2007, it was quietly removed from Qingdao's list of SOEs.[39]

Precisely because of their political obligations and structure, SOEs are not a major source of private accumulation. Relatives of Party officials, including the sons of Hu Jintao and Wen Jiabao, are indeed making huge fortunes—but in private equity rather than the central state sector. Indeed, the activities of such "little emperors" are regarded as a threat by those families (especially the "red-blooded" revolutionary dynasties) who do not have their fingers in the private-sector pie.[40] Compensation for even senior managers in the state sector is comparatively low.[41] Nor is it the case, even formally, that state managers of the central enterprises are directed solely towards profit maximization. Managerial performance is often assessed on the basis of productivity, efficiency and safety indices; but shareholder-focused metrics such as stock prices, shareholder return and economic value are often absent. Moreover, clearly non-economic criteria are stressed. The performance contracts of two PetroChina vice presidents included "improving ideological work, enhancing Party conduct and anti-corruption campaign," to be met through "preventing occurrences of any mass commotion and any severe offense against Party conduct."[42] The significance of such non-economic over economic criteria became clear during the 2008-9 credit crisis and recession, when state-controlled firms were ordered not to cut jobs and spending.[43]

Yet, paradoxically, it is in relation to "letting go the small" that the primacy of profit-maximization and "capitalist principles" are most questionable. Unlike the central government, local governments (from counties up to provinces) in the 1990s still ran enterprises across a wide range of industrial sectors. Consequently, their factories were smaller and more vulnerable to competitive pressures.[44] As a whole, the state-owned small and medium enterprises were losing money. It was expected that, given the pull of greater authority and push of harder budget constraints, local governments would embrace the solution of privatization. Many did, and between 1998 and 2012 the number of SOEs was reduced by half, from approximately 300,000 to 145,000. Given their much larger share of overall state sector employment, the privatizations and lay-offs at these firms accounted for the vast majority of job losses during this period.[45] These lay-offs, more than any other single factor, likely contributed to the plummeting income share of wages and depressed consumption that has now garnered so much attention.[46] Household consumption as a proportion of GDP fell from 72 percent in 1992 to 35 percent in 2011.[47] Fully 39 percent of urban households reported a drop in income in 1997.[48] Many of these unemployed workers, Alvin So suggests, have not been fully proletarianized because they maintain an "off-duty" (*xiagang*) status with their former employer, entailing regular livelihood allowances and, crucially, retention of former work-unit housing.[49] Still, the livelihood allowances are a pittance and likely ensure only bare subsistence.

Distinguishing between reform outcomes in the "large" (natural resource and capital-intensive) and "small" (labor-intensive and industrially diversified) state sectors helps to explain why the state's total share of output and fixed investment remains high even as its share of employment has declined dramatically, and why output in most manufacturing ("downstream") sectors is now dominated by private and even foreign capital.[50] Even after large-scale privatization, though, tens of thousands of SOEs have been maintained at local levels. Are they "winners" in the economic competition, as Andreas suggests? On the whole, the *opposite* is the case. The policy measures of the late 1990s *did* inaugurate a mass "shakeout" of small and medium SOEs but the process was never completed.[51] In fact, remaining local SOE managers have continued to reproduce themselves and their firms through old methods: extensive growth facilitated by local protectionism, soft budget constraints, and mounting NPLs. Understanding how and why this is so is vital for fully assessing the extent to which capitalist social property relations have been restored in China.

Patterns of 'malign' redistribution

The depressed domestic consumption levels that followed from SOE and TVE privatization had highly differential effects on the profitability of Chinese firms. Those in the export-oriented sector, where both foreign-invested and Chinese privately-owned firms are concentrated, garnered reliable profits because they found a source of demand in the world market. As capitalist firms, their reproduction depended on producing competitively—and they proved especially adept at doing so by combining cheap migrant labor with advanced industrial technique.[52] Earnings from China's export sector swelled Beijing's foreign exchange reserves, as capital and currency controls prevented outflows of capital and appreciation of the currency. The recycling of these foreign exchange earnings, especially through the purchase of US Treasury bills, facilitated access to cheap credit by American households and the continued purchase of Chinese-produced consumer goods. This cycle contributed to the expansion of both economies until the credit crisis and ensuing recession of 2008.

Local SOEs largely lacked the advanced technology and technique required for competitive production in the world market, restricting them to domestic market-oriented production. Given the overcapacity that existed in the state sector before restructuring and the depressed demand conditions that prevailed afterwards, it is little surprise that local governments resorted to privatization and fostering competitive capitalist enterprises. Yet, the remaining SOEs have continued their pattern of making excessive and unprofitable fixed investments in such sectors as steel, automobiles, cement and aluminum. These investments have been facilitated by a number of factors. Ho-fung Hung, in an insightful analysis of this phenomenon, partly blames the "underdevelopment" of the financial market, making it difficult for enterprises to divert their savings to invest in underdeveloped sectors that might yield higher profits. While potentially important, this lack of profit-making opportunity does not explain why unprofitable SOEs have been able to survive *despite* their losses. The underlying reason is simple — because they can! As Hung notes:

> Major state-owned banks, rather than discipline enterprises and direct them away from excessive and low return investments, encourage these investments though lax lending practices. These banks, as the financial arms of the central and local governments, deliver easy credits to insolvent or profligate state-owned industrial enterprises, of which roughly 40 percent incurred losses in 2006, according to government figures. In contrast, private enterprises, even very successful ones, are at a disadvantageous position in obtaining financial support from major state banks. The irony that losing state enterprises can obtain credit more easily than profitable and promising private enterprises sets China apart from the developmental experiences of other East Asian developmental states, where state funded industrial banks

allocate resources to the 'winners', not the 'losers'.[53]

In fact, these bank loans essentially act as a channel for the "malign redistribution" of financial resources.[54] Profit-making economic units deposit their savings into the banks and pay taxes to the government, which are then funnelled to loss-making SOEs. Consequently, the problem of NPLs—which the restructuring reforms were supposed to vanquish—has hardly disappeared. The ratio of non-performing loans to all outstanding loans has fallen since the late 1990s, but only through a process of recurrent governmental overhauls and bailouts. Existing NPLs are transferred to state-owned asset management companies, even as new loans are expanded. State banks continued to lend without taking into account the profitability and risk of their borrowers.[55] Indeed, it is likely that they have studiously avoided implementing the necessary monitoring mechanisms "so that they do not cut off the capital supply to non-profit-making SOEs."[56]

This is a truly curious phenomenon, and it departs dramatically from what the CCP leadership intended to enact through restructuring. How is it to be explained? Hung maintains that the pattern of malign redistribution results from the aggregate result of local developmental state efforts, entailing "anarchic competition among localities" and the uncoordinated construction of redundant production capacity.[57] While decentralization is an important factor, it does not explain why local officials have been able to sustain this unprofitable pattern. Why have the banks enabled it, despite reforms that were supposed to "commercialize" their decision-making? Why have senior officials allowed it, despite a "cadre responsibility system" that is supposed to privilege profitability? We can only provide a comprehensive answer if we question Hung's thesis that China has become a "capitalist authoritarian state, which defends the private accumulation of capital and guards the interests of its beneficiaries against any resistance from below."[58] In fact, the pattern of malign redistribution results from an *incomplete* transition to capitalist authoritarianism, insofar as the party-state has been unable to fully transform bureaucratic-collectivist social property relations. On the one hand, workers have resisted their dispossession through significant if disconnected struggles, invoking the socialist principles that the regime supposedly defends. On the other hand, officials and managers at various levels have sought to defend their politically-constituted property, fostering partially concealed but nevertheless significant internal conflict within the bureaucracy itself.

Working class struggles and intra-bureaucratic cleavages

In his own way, Hung recognizes the importance of workers' struggles when he notes that the state banks' priority in extending loans "is to maintain social and political stability by slowing massive layoffs by [unprofitable] SOEs."[59] Behind the oft-cited regime goal of maintaining stability, however, is a genuine contestation over access to the means of production and resistance to the prospect of full market dependence. Feng Chen, a keen scholarly observer of state worker struggles, notes that "the rhetorical legacy of the past—the old socialist conception of public property—becomes one major resource used by discontented workers."[60] Focusing on the issue of public property ownership enables state workers to make two distinct types of "moral-economic" claims. The first is that workers, as the legal "master of the enterprise," must be accorded a voice in the negotiations that determine their firm's fate. In the second case, workers do not use official ideology to merely claim a place at the bargaining table; instead, they wield it to question the very legitimacy of restructuring itself. Such claims usually arise in the context of outright privatizations, in which the transfer of state assets into private hands is thought to contradict the socialist principles of public ownership. Slogans such as "Give the Factory Back to Me!" and "Reform Does Not Allow Privatization!" encapsulate the sentiment behind these claims.[61] Although aggregate data is not available, academics who have studied such protests note that state workers are very often able to derail the restructuring proposals that seem to threaten them.[62] Chen observes:

> [D]espite reforms aimed at separating the government and enterprises, local governments still have institutional leverage over SOEs. Superior bodies of these enterprises, whatever they are now called (e.g., general companies or state holding corporations), are de facto official agencies within the structure of government institutional control. Once a protest erupts, these official organs are able to exert direct and decisive influence on dispute settlements.... In the cases I gathered as well as those reported by the media, governmental agencies played a critical role in pressuring management to respond to workers' demands.[63]

Unlike private sector or unemployed workers, workers in the state sector are able to place demands upon the political economic levers of the state—levers that are legitimated by "socialist legality" and the official socialist ideology.

The relevance of workers' struggles is most obvious when considered in relation to individual enterprise restructurings. However, it stands to reason that the aggregate effect of these outbreaks—and the prospect of metastasis—served to slow and even halt restructuring agendas at various levels of government. Some observers of the course of the restructuring program have suggested that a change of course was apparent even in early 1998, with the scrapping or limitation of lay-off schedules. This was partly due to concerns over reverberations from the 1997 Asian crisis; but "the main reason was the upsurge in labor unrest, strikes, and protests sparked by the redundancy programme."[64] Indeed, in certain cases larger SOEs were compelled to take over loss-making enterprises, not in order to reform them or return them to profit, but simply to ensure wages and pension payments. There was thus a shift in emphasis to a "headline" reduction in workforce numbers, as sub-companies proliferated to absorb surplus labor.[65] The direct impact of workers' struggles dovetailed with broader societal influences, such as the 2004 controversy over MBOs and the growth of a New Left intellectual opposition to further capitalist reforms.[66] The overall effect has not only been the widespread maintenance of unprofitable SOEs, but also a general halt in privatization, with SOEs blocked from applying for bankruptcy by local officials.[67] In this respect, the fundamental contradiction of market socialism—between public ownership and enforcing market dependence—remains unresolved for at least a substantial section of Chinese industry.

Against this backdrop of state worker resistance there have also been significant intra-bureaucratic schisms over the extent to which market-dependent social relations (that is, capitalism) should be pushed. At the local level, of course, officials and managers have not been shy to convert themselves into cadre-capitalists, as many critical scholars have noted. Yet even in China, where "fuzzy" property rights and political connections endow cadres-capitalists with definite advantages, the opportunities of the market do not come without real risks. There are countless stories of personal enrichment through privatization, but state managers are also aware of the many cases in which the opposite has resulted. Robert Weil observes that

> many Communist Party cadre in former state-owned enterprises end up being kicked out after they have helped to sell them off to private investors. They are not kept on by the new capitalist owners, a condition that one worker described as

'burning the bridge you just crossed.' As a consequence, many of them are now also unemployed and understand better what 'marketization' is really about—'it raises their consciousness.'[68]

It is thus quite rational, despite the expansion of the capitalist market and plenty of profiteering opportunities, for managers and officials to guard their connections to politically-constituted property. Continuous access to state loans enables them to meet political criteria—profitability, tax generation and social stability—without the risks of relying on private capital accumulation or the difficulties of instituting intensive growth.[69]

At the central and leadership level, too, a number of factors have conspired to divide Party members over the wisdom of proceeding with reforms that will instantiate market dependence. Concern over long-term Party legitimacy and survival is of course central. Worker unrest is reportedly considered to be the third most worrying threat to stability for Party leaders, behind only the separatist movements in Xinjiang and Tibet.[70] Without shedding the official socialist ideals on which it has still stands, the Party has found it impossible to fully transform the state-owned industries along capitalist lines. Yet, politically-constituted property is being maintained for more than purely reactive reasons. The party-state is still exercised by the bureau-cratic-collectivist ambition of maintaining its claim on the total social surplus and directing the overall pace and pattern of development. Keeping a significant state-owned industrial sector for fixed-asset investment, and the monopoly of state banks for credit provision, has facilitated this broad goal. The party-state was therefore equipped with a rather unique set of political resources for combating the effects of the global recession. Before the downturn, many critical scholars, including Hart-Landsberg and Burkett, predicted a disaster for Beijing in the event of a significant downturn in American consumer demand.[71] Indeed, the effect *was* disastrous for the export sector itself. As many as 670,000 factories were shut down in the coastal cities of Guangdong, Dongguan and Shenzhen, and 25 million migrants lost their jobs.[72]

Yet the party-state was able to maintain GDP growth by implementing what the *Economist* characterized as "the biggest two-year stimulus in government history," directing state banks to loan, and state industries to invest, regardless of profitability concerns.[73] The resulting spasm of extensive growth not only saved China from recession, it also likely provided a crucial source of capital goods demand for much of East Asia as European and American demand plummeted.[74] In 2009, the proportion of industrial production by state companies actually increased, as SOEs not only intensified fixed investment in their own industries but also expanded into "downstream" sectors previously vacated. Private entrepreneurs refer to the process as "the state advances, the private sector retreats,"[75] while liberal economists complain of a "third wave of nationalisation."[76]

While the predictions of Hart-Landsberg and other critical scholars have not been borne out by the crisis, China is hardly set to anchor a harmonious, global "commonwealth of civilizations." From the 1980s onwards, China's ability to maintain accumulation without dispossession (that is, extensive growth through bureaucratic-collectivist social property forms) has been increasingly conditioned by its facilitation of capitalist growth—first only on the margins, then throughout the whole of the economy. Not only is capitalist growth necessary to provide the taxation and jobs that extensive state-directed growth cannot, it also provides much of the resources that are "malignly" redistributed to fuel extensive growth in the state sector. Thus, although the restructuring of the late 1990s has not yet yielded a clearly capitalist separation between the political and the economic or a thorough abandonment of politically-constituted property, the party-state clearly relies upon capitalist growth. China's response to the recession illustrates both sides of this phenomenon. On the hand, the success of Beijing's stimulus resulted from its casual abandonment of market-based, "commercial" criteria; on the other hand, the onslaught of bad debt that already appears on the horizon cannot be neutralized without the resources provided by the capitalists, especially exporters. Even as Beijing directed the banks to lend, it extended inducements to exporters and eased away from implementing the worker protections that Arrighi champions.[77]

The current impasse and emerging conflicts

Contemporary China is a far cry from what Deng initially envisioned. The pursuit of intensive, Smithian growth eventually cast much of the state sector into bankruptcy while opening the door wide to foreign capital. Both policies, in different ways, entailed a disciplining of labor and, consequently, a limitation of domestic demand. Given its current political economic structure, Beijing has little opportunity to shape an internationally competitive domestic capitalist class in the manner of Taiwan and South Korea. China's future will depend upon how this impasse is managed. Despite commonplace suggestions by liberal economists, the state sector in China has acted to maintain demand against the vagaries of market dependence.[78] A full industrial "shakeout" would have depressed overall consumption much further. Still, the market retains its magic for many, including the Chinese New Right and their liberal allies within the Party. Much as WTO entry was used by the Zhang/Zhou regime to implement domestic restructuring, the New Right and foreign economists are now pushing a "rebalancing" agenda that would imply a final dissolution of politically-constituted property: price and financial sector "liberalization," privatization of state industry, and end to capital controls.[79]

Perhaps most significant for Chinese peasants are various

proposals to achieve greater productivity in agriculture by promoting the consolidation of larger and more concentrated farms—either by privatizing land ownership outright or by promoting the commercial exchange of land use rights.[80] Liberal economists in both China and the West argue that a greater "commercialization" of agriculture will enhance rural prosperity by promoting greater "opportunities" for profit maximization through economies of scale. Some peasant activists and left intellectuals, meanwhile, regard land privatization as a positive step for preventing illegal expropriation of land use rights by township governments.[81] Since 1987, an estimated 34 million peasants have been dispossessed of their holdings, in what the Chinese business journal *Caijing* has termed a "new 'enclosure' movement."[82] Yet peasants have, in the main, defended the existing land use system through strategies of rightful resistance, raising demands like "Collectively Owned Land Should Not Be Used for Commercial Purposes."[83] Liberal ambitions to establish agrarian capitalism in China depend on the extent to which a real enclosure movement is created—not through scattered dispossessions, but through a transformation of the existing land use system to foster market dependence. Even as commercial contracting arrangements increasingly appear in the countryside, non-market access to land remains of central importance. Qian Forrest Zhang and John Donaldson have extensively investigated the nature and dynamics of these relationships, observing that:

[C]ollective ownership protects agricultural producers—to various degrees—from domination, exploitation and dispossession by outside capital. Nearly all [contracting] companies we interviewed expressed a desire to expand their production bases. The primary barrier to expanding these bases is the lack of land—or, to put it another way, the difficulty in wresting control of collective land from rural households. In fact, many companies and entrepreneurs that have formed bases have had to do so on previously unproductive, marginal land. In many other countries, battles pitting powerful corporations against unorganized small farmers have led to smallholding farmers being dispossessed. In China, farmers' protected land rights provide them with a tool to resist pressure from the companies.... An army of landless vagabonds has not emerged.[84]

It may be true in one sense, as suggested by Andreas, that the maintenance of the existing land system "serves" the broad interests of capital insofar as it acts to insulate migrant workers from the full depredations of market dependence. The millions of migrant workers laid off in 2008-9 often returned to their villages to help on family plots—a trend that actually began before the recession with the abolition of the agricultural tax and implementation of various "new socialist countryside" measures.[85] To insist on this structural interpretation, however, would be to largely miss the point. It is precisely this non-market access to the land that is an object of active contestation and debate today, including by capitalist corporations and pro-capitalist intellectuals.

Their prospect for success in the near term, however, is slim. Opinion polls peg economists as the least popular group in China, and their agenda is now even less attractive.[86] Yet they provide ready answers to questions that plague the Party and country. Even in the midst of the financial crisis, Wen Jiabao pledged to "speed up reforms" and "give full play to market forces in allocating resources."[87] Although intra-bureaucratic factionalism is kept well concealed from the outside world, questions like these have the real potential to split the Party. In March 2006, when the Party failed yet again to pass a proposed property law amidst popular and intra-party opposition, a group of fifty liberal economists, legal experts and senior government officials met secretly in Beijing to plot future strategy. As one participant put in a leaked transcript of the meeting, the participants were tired of having to "signal left while actually seeking to turn right." There were calls to adopt the Taiwanese model, for a formal split of the CCP into two factions, and even for the military to be directed by the state (rather than Party).[88]

Whether this will provide a template for future factional struggle remains to be seen. Similar demands were raised by right-wing Party members, liberal Chinese economists, and Western observers in the months before and after the CCP convened its Eighteenth National Congress in November 2012, where a Politburo Standing Committee headed by a new president, the comparatively young and charismatic Xi Jinping, was unveiled.[89] Xi hails from a so-called red-blooded dynasty— his father, Xi Zhongxun, fought alongside Mao in the 1940s and later helped to persuade Deng to make Shenzhen an SEZ in the early 1980s. Like other "princelings," Xi has an extended family that reportedly own assets worth hundreds of millions of dollars but he and his immediate family do not seem to have similar riches. In a leaked 2009 cable from the US Embassy in Beijing, Xi was described by an acquaintance as someone "repulsed by the all-encompassing commercialization of Chinese society, with its attendant nouveau riche, official corruption, loss of values, dignity, and self- respect."[90] Now that he has been elevated to the country's most powerful office, Xi pledges to continue walking the bureaucratic-collectivist tightrope, maintaining the uneasy balance between vocal liberal elements who increasingly wish to dive head first into the capitalist abyss and a renascent left-wing that wants a halt to perilous marketization measures. Giving an American twist to stale nationalist rhetoric, Xi seeks to provide a steadying vision with his new slogan "the Chinese dream," urging "the great revival of the Chinese people." He has committed, like his predecessors, to continue with gradual reforms in finance, industry and agriculture while somehow combatting corruption and curtailing inequality, aiming for the achievement of a "rich, strong, democratic, civilised and harmonious socialist society" by 2049.[91]

Behind the saccharine language lies a bitter reality. With mass protests against land grabs and other abuses numbering 180,000 in 2010,[92] Xi is aware that the Party's grip is tenuous and that too great a relaxation of its ideological and material prerequisites could be suicidal. For this reason he has made clear that the China dream is also a "strong-army dream" in which the military will remain obedient to Party dictates, rejecting calls in some quarters for a speedier transition to "constitutionalism." In unpublished remarks made during a trip to southern China in December 2012, Xi also reportedly raised the ominous precedent of Soviet end days, warning: "The Chinese dream is an ideal. Communists should have a higher ideal, and that is Communism." Nearly a quarter century after Deng seized on the same experience to justify an expansion of market reforms in order to preserve Party power, the CCP leadership is still unable to square the circle of market socialism. Xi's China dream, like previous incarnations of Chinese market socialism, will only prove a pipe dream. Future inter- and intra-class struggles of some form are guaranteed, and will determine the ultimate fate of remaining non-capitalist social property forms. The biggest question is whether workers and peasants will mobilize independently of various Party factions and pro-capitalist ideologues, reclaiming the "higher ideal" of communism from a ruling Party that abandoned it long before 1949.

Chapter Seven

Conclusion

The principal objective of this book was to assess China's status and potential as a non-capitalist model of development. That it is worth querying China's status in this regard may have come as a surprise to some. By the early 2000s the one-time boosters of Chinese market socialism had largely fallen by the wayside. Certainly, it seemed, any weary defenders left standing on the intellectual battlefield were dealt a merciless *coup de grace* by Hart-Landsberg and Burkett's piercing polemic. Arrighi's *Adam Smith in Beijing* did not overturn this consensus, at least among Marxists. It did, however, ask pertinent questions about the degree to which accumulation with dispossession (that is, primitive accumulation) had advanced within China. Perhaps more importantly, it displayed a refreshing willingness to engage with broad theoretical and historical issues, particularly concerning the distinguishing characteristics of markets, capitalism, and the capitalist state. That Arrighi largely gets these issues wrong—and leads us in a deeply problematic theoretical direction—is perhaps less important than the fact that he asks the right questions.

This book departed from the suggestion that analytical contradictions between *China and Socialism* and *Adam Smith in Beijing* reflect real contradictions in China's reform process. Hart-Landsberg and Burkett, and the many critical scholars who have embraced their work, are certainly correct to stress the inherent problems of any attempt to craft market socialism, and the particularly negative ramifications of Beijing's attempt to do so for Chinese workers. That market reforms have brought China very far from socialism while establishing a vast new terrain for the sway of capitalist imperatives is well established in *China and*

Socialism. Yet Arrighi's contention that significant forms of what he terms "accumulation without dispossession" prevail into the present, and that there remains an open-ended quality to political economic conflict in China, remains compelling. Peasant access to agricultural land, and the sizeable role of state-owned industry, requires serious attention by historical materialists. The challenge, to paraphrase Marx, is to identify the concepts and categories that are most useful for reproducing "in thought" the "real concrete" complexities of contemporary China.

A critical overview of both works establishes that the central categories of capitalism and socialism are left vague or incorrectly understood. To understand the first, it was proposed that we return to debates surrounding the transition to capitalism to uncover its specificity as a social form. Both Arrighi, by emphasizing the necessity of direct state control by capitalists, and Hart-Landsberg and Burkett, by relying on a rather abstract model of generalized commodity production, reproduce certain flawed conceptions of capitalism found within the broadly Marxist tradition. Brenner's focus on the loss of direct, non-market access to the means of production by producers and appropriators alike offers a crucial corrective because it refuses to naturalize capitalism or identify it with ancient commercial practices. Instead, the laws of motion specific to capitalism arose first in England as an unintended consequence of class struggles and subsequently spread throughout the world in a geopolitically-mediated way, adapting and transforming a vast array of pre-capitalist social structures. In this light, the CCP's decisions to pursue "socialization" of industry and agriculture in the 1950s, and market reforms in the late 1970s, were both facets of a much broader process of global combined and uneven development.

Understanding the specificity of capitalism provides useful insights in the other "transition" debate. If we employ a Marxist vision of socialism as entailing high levels of labor productivity for the realization of generalized abundance, it is quite clear that China *never* constituted a socialist alternative, even at the height of Maoist mobilizations. This is not simply a normatively convenient claim: it is central to recognizing the specific form of non-capitalist social property relations in China, the class dynamics these relations inscribed, and the external and internal contradictions they engendered. The path to socialism in China, while historically open in the 1920s, was narrowed in subsequent decades as the CCP committed itself to the nationalist aims of "socialism in one country" and actively suppressed any prospect of genuine workers' democracy. These moves prevented the achievement of conditions that Marx regarded as essential for obtaining high labor productivity through non-capitalist means: specifically, the inheritance of advanced technology and technique available in advanced capitalist countries, and institutions of workers' democracy to promote effective economic planning.

Maoist China and other Soviet-type societies are therefore best understood through the prism of bureaucratic-collectivist social property relations, an analysis that is most consistent with the historicization of capitalism developed here. The Communist Party bureaucracy can indeed constitute a distinct exploiting class by using forms of politically-constituted property for surplus extraction. This runs counter to Trotskyist deformed workers' state analysis, which typically asserts that the bureaucracy only constitutes a parasitic caste rather than an exploiting class. Nevertheless, many Trotskyist insights can and should be given serious attention, including the heterogeneous and factionalized character of the bureaucracy and the way in which official socialist ideology may be utilized by direct producers in political contestation. There is a crucial difference between bureaucratic collectivism and other non-capitalist class societies in which ruling class surplus extraction was conditioned by property in the state (e.g., absolutism). In the latter, the state was literally the private property of the monarch, alienated to officials, and legitimated by notions of divine right. In the former, it is the Communist (or equivalent) Party that owns the state, appoints officials, and is legitimated by claims to socialist ideals.

The primary analytical and political question for assessing China's status as a non-capitalist alternative is therefore the extent to which bureaucratic-collectivist social property relations persist into the present. Given the absence of institutions of workers' democracy in bureaucratically planned economies, strategies of extensive growth through non-capitalist mechanisms were highly successful in the short term, but eventually ran into inherent barriers. In aiming to resolve these problems while maintaining their own privileges, party-state bureaucracies have historically sought to achieve intensive growth with the introduction of market mechanisms. As political Marxists have argued, however, the self-sustaining efficiency gains typically associated with the market are in fact specifically capitalist, and cannot be obtained without reducing producers and appropriators to market dependence. The first decade or more of the reform era in China provides ample illustration of this. Without forcing bankruptcy, SOEs continued patterns of extensive growth while using the market as an opportunity for profiteering. Intensive, capitalist growth patterns were only established by privately-owned enterprises (foreign-invested and small-scale domestic Chinese). The TVEs that garnered so much enthusiasm by market socialists and liberals alike were a half-way house between these two sectors: producing for increasingly competitive markets but constituted by, and ultimately dependent upon, local governments. Their almost wholesale collapse as collectively-owned enterprises was ultimately conditioned by decisions at higher political levels to impose "hard budgets" and force bankruptcy.

Since Deng's 1992 "Southern Tour," the party-state has sought to overcome the failure of previous reform efforts by enabling a massive expansion of the private (especially export-oriented) sector, while extending bankruptcy and "hard budget constraints" to unprofitable SOEs. The cumulative effect of these policies, and the social toll they have exacted on direct producers, provide the basis for Hart-Landsberg and Burkett's claim that a "full-blown" capitalism has been restored in China. Many of the ills they point to are, unfortunately, undeniable and harrowing facets of China's recent development story: super-exploitation of migrant labor, the loss of the "iron rice bowl," mass privatization, increasing dependence on exports and foreign investments, and primitive accumulation and the emergence of a cadre-capitalist class. These facts are either ignored by current champions of China, or simply regarded as unavoidable or inevitable by-products of modernization. Marxists critics are absolutely correct to insist that they are not.

Still, in recognizing these facts, there is no need to insist that capitalism is "full blown" and completely restored, that "capitalist principles" govern nearly all enterprises, and that peasants have been dispossessed. This book has shown that in both agriculture and state industry, direct non-market access to the means of production by producers and appropriators (managers and officials) remains. The 1997 restructuring program was a grand attempt to finally transform state industry through a massive "shakeout" of unprofitable enterprises and the reorganisation of corporate governance in central SOEs and state banks. It appeared, in short, to be a capitalist counter-revolution from above perpetrated by the state class. To a large extent a shakeout was achieved, engendering mass layoffs and a significant diminution of aggregate consumption—the consequences of which are very much present even today in discussions of economic rebalancing. Yet struggles and conflicts between classes and within the ruling class acted to frustrate a full transition to market-dependent reproduction. Tens of thousands of unprofitable SOEs are still maintained, and in fact favoured by state banks. Worker struggles in state industry, the opposition of local officials and managers to privatization, and central government concerns for legitimacy have all been important and interrelated factors in yielding this impasse.

The party-state's unwillingness to place itself in a position of structural dependence on the capitalist class is an important aspect of recent intra-party debates. The wisdom of maintaining such autonomy was undoubtedly confirmed for many Party members during the recent recession. Beijing was able to maintain economic expansion through massive extensive growth, as migrant workers laid off in the privately-owned export sector returned to the countryside. It is here where China's status as a non-capitalist alternative is readily apparent: bureaucratic-collectivist social property relations remain central in the overall dynamics of the Chinese political economy, insulating key sectors from market dependence. Yet, the severe limitations of this alternative are also clear. Beijing's ability to maintain unprofitable, extensive growth patterns in the reform period has only been facilitated by the expansion of capitalist enterprises, which provide both jobs and tax revenue. The party-state can mobilize politically-constituted property to compensate for capitalist losses in the short term; in the long term, however, the party-state is increasingly compelled to expand the field of capitalization. International and domestic policy debates carry profound implications for the future of non-capitalist social property relations in China. Their resolution will shape the future of millions of direct producers, and the historical legacy of the Chinese Revolution itself.

Before ending, it is important to more explicitly clarify the political implications of the analysis offered here. Arrighi is justly criticized by many Marxists for prettifying the Chinese developmental model in a vain search for practical, really-existing alternatives to American capitalist hegemony. Before China emerged, it was supposedly Japan that had the potential to inaugurate an end to capitalist history.[1] Arrighi's pessimism at the prospect of a socialist future, and his deep revulsion for imperialist domination, compelled him to seek alternatives to capitalism where they do not exist and to fundamentally misunderstand the dynamics of capitalism itself. Hart-Landsberg and Burkett, in contrast, are insistent that socialism offers the only genuine alternative to capitalist developmental models and seek to expose the anti-working class implications of market relations, from Japan, to Korea, and now to China.[2] Yet, in doing so, they are often eager to intervene in debates among "progressive" scholars and policy makers. An animating concern for writing *China and Socialism*, for example, was to dissuade Cuba from following China in implementing market reforms. This concern is entirely justified in light of Cuba's recent intentions to axe up to one million state jobs, reducing the state sector from 85 percent to 65 percent of GDP by 2015.[3] In their rush to scratch China off the list of progressive models, however, they ignore the country's remaining non-capitalist social property relations, and don't fully comprehend why Cuba—like China—has chosen to wander down the market path.

The analysis presented here, however, has highlighted the traditional Marxist understanding of socialism to call attention to the *inherent* limitations of all national "models" of development, particularly those predicated upon bureaucratic-collectivist property forms. It has illuminated the contradictory dynamics compelling Communist Party bureaucracies to adopt market reforms, as well as the class struggles that have prevented the full imposition of capitalist social property relations. This leads to an important clarification of an observation made by the respected Left scholar Leo Panitch, who writes that Communist Party rule "still acts like an albatross on the working classes, severely restraining class-struggles and most certainly not providing revolutionary inspiration for such struggles."[4] In one respect this is absolutely correct. The Party was an albatross even before 1949 and actively prevented workers' democracy. However, we must also recognize that after 1949 the CCP did implement non-capitalist social property forms, which even today the working classes in China have sought to defend and extend. Political interventions in China (and Cuba) should proceed from this fact, while insisting on the necessity of workers' democracy domestically and internationally as the only means for achieving an authentic and viable socialism.

Notes

Chapter One

1. Perry Anderson, "Two Revolutions," *New Left Review*, II/61 (January/February 2010), 59.

2. Minqi Li, *The Rise of China and the Demise of the Capitalist World Economy* (New York: Monthly Review, 2008), 66.

3. Cf. Victor D. Lippit, "But What about China?", *Rethinking Marxism* 6:1 (Spring 1993): 128-13; John Roemer, *A Future for Socialism* (Cambridge, MA: Harvard University Press, 1994), 126-128.

4. Gerard Greenfield and Apo Leong, "China's Communist Capitalism: The Real World of Market Socialism," in *Socialist Register 1997: Ruthless Criticism of All That Exists*, ed. Leo Panitch (London: Merlin, 1997), 115. An engaging summary of this debate can be found in Bertell Ollman (ed.), *Market Socialism: The Debate Among Socialists* (New York: Routledge, 1998); see also Robin Blackburn (ed.), *After the Fall: The Failure of Communism and the Future of Socialism* (London: Verso, 1991).

5. Hart-Landsberg and Burkett's essay was originally published in a special book-length issue of *Monthly Review* (July-August 2004) and later issued as a stand-alone book under the Monthly Review Press imprint. Further references to this work here correspond to page numbers in the July-August 2004 issue of *Monthly Review*. For extensions of their analysis, see Hart-Landsberg and Burkett, "China and the Dynamics of Transnational Accumulation: Causes and Consequences of Global Restructuring," *Historical Materialism* 14:3 (2006): 3-43; Hart-Landsberg and Burkett, "China, Capitalist Accumulation, and Labor," *Monthly Review* 59:1 (May 2007): 17-39; Hart-Landsberg, "China, Capitalist Accumulation and the World Crisis," *Marxism* 21 (South Korea, no date given):

271-297; Hart-Landsberg, "The U.S. Economy and China," *Monthly Review* 61:9 (February 2010): 14-21; and Hart-Landsberg, "The Chinese Reform Experience: A Critical Assessment," *Review of Radical Political Economics* 43:1 (March 2011): 56-76.

6. See especially the January 2005 issue of *Critical Asian Studies* (37:3), devoted to discussions of *China and Socialism*; issue 18.1 of *Historical Materialism* (2010), containing a symposium on *Adam Smith in Beijing*; and Joel Andreas, "Changing Colours in China," *New Left Review* II/54 (November-December 2008): 123-142.

7. Hart-Landsberg and Burkett, *China and Socialism*, 9.

8. Arrighi, *Adam Smith in Beijing*, 353.

9. *Ibid.*, 389.

10. Minqi Li combines Arrighi's world systems theory with a restoration thesis that is similar to *Monthly Review*'s. See Li, *The Rise of China and the Demise of the Capitalist World Economy* (New York: Monthly Review Press, 2008), chapters 4 and 5; and "The Rise of the Working Class and the Future of the Chinese Revolution," *Monthly Review* 63:2 (June 2011). See also the essays collected in Ho-fung Hung (ed.), *China and the Transformation of Global Capitalism* (Baltimore: John Hopkins University Press, 2009), many of which employ a world systems theoretic approach similar to, or directly inspired by, Arrighi's.

11. Lin Chun, a formidable defender of what she calls Chinese "modest prosperity" socialism, makes reference to Arrighi and the Braudelian conception of capitalism while omitting any broader world systemic apparatus. See Chun, "Challenging Privatization: A Conceptual and Theoretical Argument," *Chinese Journal of Political Science* 14 (2009): 21-48; and Chun, *The Transformation of Chinese Socialism* (Durham: Duke University Press, 2006).

12. Yiching Wu, "Rethinking China's Capitalist Restoration,"

Monthly Review 57:6 (November 2005): 44-63; Flemming Christiansen, "Arrighi's *Adam Smith in Beijing*: Engaging China," *Historical Materialism* 18:1 (2010), 124-6.

13. Anderson, "Two Revolutions," 95.

14. While the Soviet Union certainly experienced a counter-revolution, to what extent its social property relations have been adjusted in a genuinely capitalist direction remains an open and contested question. See David Kotz, "Is Russia Becoming Capitalist?", *Science & Society* 65:2 (Summer 2001): 157-181; David Lane, "Global Capitalism and the Transformation of State Socialism," *Studies in Comparative International Development* 44 (2009): 97-117; and Simon Clarke, *The Development of Capitalism in Russia* (London: Routledge, 2006). On Moscow's mass privatization of state assets, see Chrystia Freeland, *Sale of the Century: Russia's Wild Ride from Communism to Capitalism* (Toronto: Doubleday, 2000).

Chapter Two

1. Jonathan Anderson, "How to Think about China," *Asian Economic Perspectives* (UBS Investment Research), January 2006, 3.

2. Elizabeth Perry, "Reclaiming the Chinese Revolution," *Journal of Asian Studies* 67:4 (November 2008): 1148-1149. For an outstanding example of Perry's historical work, see Elizabeth Perry and Li Xun, *Proletarian Power: Shanghai in the Cultural Revolution* (Boulder: Westview, 1997).

3. Mark Selden, *The Yenan Way in Revolutionary China* (Cambridge, MA: Harvard University Press, 1971), viii.

4. Edward Friedman, "The Innovator," in *Mao-Tse Tung in the Scales of History*, ed. Dick Wilson (New York: Cambridge University Press, 1977).

5. Edward Friedman, Paul Pickowicz, and Mark Selden, *Revolution, Resistance, and Reform in Village China* (New

Haven: Yale University Press, 2005), 125.

6. Edward Friedman, "How Economic Superpower Could Transform Africa," *Journal of Chinese Political Science* 14 (2009): 1-20.

7. *Fanshen* (New York: Random House, 1966) is a lengthy account of the Chinese Revolution in a single Chinese village, Long Bow. For Hinton's critique of Selden, Friedman, and many other latter-day betrayers of the Chinese Revolution, see *Through a Glass Darkly: U.S. Views of the Chinese Revolution* (New York: Monthly Review Press, 2006). See also Robert Weil, "Were Revolutions in China Necessary?", *Socialism and Democracy* 21:2 (July 2007): 1-36.

8. For examples of this "idealized" Maoism, see E.L. Wheelwright and Bruce McFarlane, *The Chinese Road to Socialism* (New York: Monthly Review Press, 1970); Maria Antonietta Macciocchi, *Daily Life in Revolutionary China* (New York: Monthly Review Press, 1972).

9. William Hinton, "The Chinese Revolution: Was it Necessary? Was it Successful? Is it Still Going On?", *Monthly Review* 43:6 (November 1991): 10-11. This makes for an interesting comparison with Hinton's statement in 1972: "China has not changed color. The working class still holds power and the Chinese people are still advancing down a revolutionary socialist road. In the coming period they will strive to transform both the economic base and the superstructure of Chinese society to suit the working class and all working people." See William Hinton, *Turning Point in China* (New York: Monthly Review Press, 1972).

10. Li, *The Rise of China*, 58.

11. Maurice Meisner, *Mao Zedong: An Intellectual and Political Portrait* (Cambridge, UK: Polity, 2007), 197-8.

12. Cf. Victor Lippit, "Socialist Development in China," in *The Transition to Socialism in China*, ed. Mark Selden and Victor Lippit (New York: M.E. Sharpe, 1982), 116-158.

13. Lippit, "The political economy," 444, 446.

14. Hart-Landsberg and Burkett, *China and Socialism*, 9.

15. Martin Hart-Landsberg and Paul Burkett, "China and the Dynamics of Transnational Accumulation: Causes and Consequences of Global Restructuring," *Historical Materialism* 14:3 (2006), 39.

16. Hart-Landsberg and Burkett, *China and Socialism*, 110.

17. *Ibid.*, 10.

18. *Ibid.*, 11. In a more recent contribution Hart-Landsberg added some meat to the bones, identifying the goals of socialism as "the promotion of all-rounded human development; solidaristic relations; co-operative planning and production for community needs; and collective or social ownership of productive assets." See "China, Capitalist Accumulation and the World Crisis," 292.

19. Arrighi, *Adam Smith in Beijing*, 16 fn 8. One "Western leftist," Naomi Klein, claims that Deng Xiaoping's market reforms led to the consolidation of a "corporate-based economy," and that it "wasn't Communism [Deng] was protecting with his [Tiananmen] crackdown, but capitalism." *The Shock Doctrine: The Rise of Disaster Capitalism* (Toronto: Knopf Canada, 2007), 221-227.

20. See the contributions in *Historical Materialism* 18:1 (2010) and Andreas, "Changing Colours in China," *New Left Review* II/54 (November-December 2008): 123-142.

21. Hart-Landsberg and Burkett, *China and Socialism*, 8.

22. *Ibid.*, 28.

23. *Ibid.*, 30.

24. Mao's "capitalist road" analysis is repeated in Harry Magdoff and John Bellamy Foster's foreword to *China and Socialism* (p.4). For an unfortunate example of how this dogma can diminish the work of otherwise compelling authors, see Li, *The Rise of China*, especially chapter 2; and Mobo Gao, *The Battle for China's Past: Mao and the Cultural*

Revolution (London: Pluto, 2008), 177.

25. Hart-Landsberg and Burkett, *China and Socialism*, 31.
26. *Ibid.* See also Hart-Landsberg, "China, Capitalist Accumulation and the World Crisis," 274: "The 'slippery slope' of market reforms thus led to an eventual privileging of market dynamics over planning, private ownership over public ownership, and foreign enterprises over domestic ones."
27. Hart-Landsberg and Burkett, *China and Socialism*, 45.
28. *Ibid.*, 67. For Liu Yufan's original article, see "A preliminary report on China's capitalist restoration," *Links: International Journal of Socialist Renewal*, no date given. URL: http://links.org.au/node/87#Accession%20to%20World%20Trade%20Organisation
29. *Ibid.*, 109.
30. *Ibid.*, 76, 75.
31. Robert Weil, "Conditions of the Working Classes in China," *Monthly Review* 58:2 (June 2006): 25.
32. See Robert Weil, "'To be attacked by the enemy is a good thing': The struggle over the legacy of Mao Zedong and the Chinese socialist revolution," *Socialism and Democracy* 20:2 (July 2006): 19-53. For the biography in question, see Jung Chang and Jon Halliday, *Mao: The Unknown Story* (London: Vintage, 2007). Weil's most substantial analysis of Chinese market socialism is *Red Cat, White Cat: China and the Contradictions of "Market Socialism"* (New York: Monthly Review Press, 1996).
33. Weil, "'To be attacked...'", 33.
34. Bruce Gilley and Heike Holbig, "The Debate on Party Legitimacy in China: a mixed quantitative/qualitative analysis," *Journal of Contemporary China* 18: 59 (2009): 347.
35. Arrighi, *Adam Smith in Beijing*, 378.
36. Andreas, "Changing Colours in China," 125. A landmark contribution in this regard is Arrighi's "World Income

Inequalities and the Future of Socialism," *New Left Review* I/189 (September-October 1991): 39-65. For Arrighi's recent work dealing with similar concerns, see Arrighi, Po-Keung Hui, Ho-Fung Hung and Mark Selden, "Historical Capitalism, East and West," in *The Resurgence of East Asia: 500, 150 and 50 year Perspectives*, ed. Arrighi et al. (New York: Routledge, 2003), 259-333; Arrighi and Beverley J. Silver, *Chaos and Governance in the World System* (Minneapolis: University of Minnesota Press, 1999); Arrighi, *The Long Twentieth Century: Money, Power and the Origins of Our Times* (London: Verso, 1994).

37. Arrighi, "The Winding Paths of Capital: Interview by David Harvey," *New Left Review* II/56 (March-April 2009), 65.

38. John S. Saul, *The Next Liberation Struggle: Capitalism, Socialism and Democracy in Southern Africa* (Toronto: Between the Lines, 2005), 8, 266. See also the collection of essays in Giovanni Arrighi and John S. Saul (eds.), *Essays on the Political Economy of Africa* (New York: Monthly Review, 1973).

39. Arrighi, "The Winding Paths of Capital," 94.

40. Sujian Guo, "Designing Market Socialism: Trustees of State Property," *Critique* 36-37 (2005), 222; see also Janos Kornai and Yingyi Qian (eds.), *Market and Socialism: In the Light of the Experiences of China and Vietnam* (New York: Palgrave, 2009).

41. See Guo, "Designing Market Socialism." Of course, this is a very simplified characterization; there are a profusion of market socialist models, a number of which are discussed in Roemer.

42. Arrighi, *Adam Smith in Beijing*, 17.

43. *Ibid.*, 25.

44. *Ibid.*, 68.

45. *Ibid.*, 43.

46. *Ibid.*, 47, 65.

47. Arrighi, *The Long Twentieth Century*, 24.

48. Arrighi, *Adam Smith in Beijing*, 92.

49. *Ibid.*, 86. See Karl Marx, *Capital,* Volume One (Harmondsworth: Pelican, 1976), 915: "The different moments of primitive accumulation can be assigned in particular to Spain, Portugal, Holland, France and England, in more or less chronological order."
50. Arrighi, *Adam Smith in Beijing,* 90-91.
51. *Ibid.*, 330-3. Like Pomeranz, James Hobson and other prominent global historians and historical sociologists, Arrighi is strongly critical of "Eurocentric" accounts of the Great Divergence that imply the West was inherently superior to the East. But their alternative, "anti-Eurocentric" narratives also rely upon some of the most problematic concepts and assumptions found in Marx and Weber's writings, including the "bourgeois" character of capitalism. See Gary Blank, "Challenging or Reinforcing the Reigning Paradigm? The Paradox of Conventional Anti-Eurocentrism," *Entremons: UPF Journal of World History,* 3 (June 2012).
52. Christopher Chase-Dunn, "*Adam Smith in Beijing*: A World Systems Perspective," *Historical Materialism* 18:1 (2010): 45.
53. Arrighi, *Adam Smith in Beijing,* 369.
54. Arrighi, *Adam Smith in Beijing,* 359.
55. Leo Panitch, "Giovanni Arrighi in Beijing: An Alternative to Capitalism?", *Historical Materialism* 18:1 (2010): 83. See also Leo Panitch and Sam Ginden, *The Making of Global Capitalism* (London: Verso, 2012), 292-300.
56. Arrighi, *Adam Smith in Beijing,* 365.
57. *Ibid.*, 24. Samir Amin, "China, Market Socialism, and U.S. Hegemony," *Review* 28:3 (2005): 259-79. Amin recently reiterated the enduring importance of common (non-private) land in contemporary Chinese villages, writing: "This 'Chinese specificity'—whose consequences are of major importance—absolutely prevents us from character-izing contemporary China (even in 2013) as 'capitalist'

because the capitalist road is based on the transformation of land into a commodity." See "China 2013," *Monthly Review* 64:10 (March 2013).

58. *Ibid.*, 363.
59. *Ibid.*, 356.
60. *Ibid.*, 369.
61. *Ibid.*, 376.
62. *Ibid.*, 368.
63. Errors in their treatment are further elaborated below.
64. *Ibid.*, 374.
65. *Ibid.*, 373.
66. *Ibid.*, 389.

Chapter Three

1. Alvin Y. So, "Beyond the Logic of Capital and the Polarization Model," *Critical Asian Studies* 37:3 (January 2005): 483.
2. For a critique of the ahistorical tendencies of Marxist economics, see Samuel Knafo, "Political Marxism and Value Theory: Bridging the Gap between Theory and History," *Historical Materialism* 15:2 (2007): 75-104.
3. See Richard Walker and Daniel Buck, "The Chinese Road: Cities in the Transition to Capitalism," *New Left Review* II/46 (July-August 2007): 39-66.
4. Richard Walker, "Karl Marx between Two Worlds: The Antimonies of Giovanni Arrighi's *Adam Smith in Beijing*," *Historical Materialism* 18:1 (2010): 59.
5. *Ibid.*, 52, 59.
6. Robert Brenner, "Bourgeois Revolution and Transition to Capitalism," in *The First Modern Society: Essays in English History in Honor of Lawrence Stone*, ed. A.L. Bier et al. (Cambridge, UK: Cambridge University Press, 1989). See also, Gary Blank, "Gender, Production, and 'the Transition to Capitalism': Assessing the Historical Basis for a Unitary

Materialist Theory," *New Proposals: Journal of Marxism and Interdisciplinary Inquiry*, 4:2 (2011): 6-28.

7. See Brenner, "Bourgeois Revolution," 272.

8. For Marx's own account, see his and Engels famous passages in the "Manifesto of the Communist Party," in Marx and Engels, *Selected Works*, Volume One (Moscow: Progress Publishers, 1961), especially pp. 108-119. For a critique, see Brenner, "Bourgeois Revolution"; George C. Comninel, *Rethinking the French Revolution: Marxism and the Revisionist Challenge* (London: Verso, 1987), chapters 3 and 7; and Comninel, "Historical Materialist Sociology and Revolutions," in *Handbook of Historical Sociology*, ed. Gerard Delanty and Engin F. Isin (London: Sage, 2003), 85-95.

9. See the relevant passages in Anderson's *Lineages of the Absolutist State* (London: Verso, 1979), especially chapter 1. Anderson's observation has been approvingly cited by certain liberal economic historians, such as Tom Bethell in *The Noblest Triumph: Property and Prosperity through the Age* (New York: St. Martin's Press, 1998), 61.

10. See Paul Sweezy's contributions to the "Transition Debate" of the 1950s, collected in Rodney Hilton (ed.), *The Transition from Feudalism to Capitalism* (London: Verso, 1978), 33-56, 102-8.

11. On this, see Robert Brenner, "The Social Basis of Economic Development" in *Analytical Marxism*, ed. John Roemer (Cambridge, UK: Cambridge University Press, 1986); also Brenner, "Property and Progress," p. 56-9; and Wood, *The Origin*, chapter 1.

12. Arrighi, *Adam Smith in Beijing*, 333.

13. For a critique, see Wood, *The Origin*, chapter 2.

14. See Karl Marx, *Capital*, Volume 1 (Harmondsworth: Penguin, 1976), chapters 27-29.

15. The essay itself and a number of critical responses can be found in see T.H. Aston and C.H.E. Philpin (eds.), *The*

Brenner Debate: Agrarian Class Structure and Economic Development in Pre-Industrial Europe (Cambridge, UK: Cambridge University Press, 2005).

16. Brenner, "Property and Progress," 58. See also Gary Blank, "Rethinking the 'Other Transition': Towards an Alternative Marxist Explanation," *Science & Society*, 77:2 (April 2013): 153-178.

17. In addition to the citations of Brenner already provided, see George C. Comninel, "English Feudalism and the Origins of Capitalism," *Journal of Peasant Studies* 27:4 (July 2000): 1-53.

18. Teschke, *The Myth of 1648: Class, Geopolitics, and the Making of Modern International Relations* (London: Verso, 2003), chapter 5.

19. *Ibid.*, 171.

20. Mike Zmolek, "Further Thoughts on Agrarian Capitalism: A Reply to Albritton," *Journal of Peasant Studies*, 29:1 (October 2001), 136.

21. Patriquin, "The Agrarian Origins of the Industrial Revolution in England," *Review of Radical Political Economics* 36:2 (Spring 2004): 204.

22. *Ibid.*, Patriquin, 206-8.

23. On this point, see Comninel, *Rethinking the French Revolution: Marxism and the Revisionist Challenge* (London: Verso, 1987), 192-3.

24. Wood, "Contradiction: Only in Capitalism" in *Socialist Register 2002: A World of Contradictions*, ed. Leo Panitch and Colin Leys (London: Merlin, 2001), 284. See also Wood, *The Origin*, 131.

25. See Wood's discussion of "empires of commerce" in *Empire of Capital* (London, Verso, 2005), 63.

26. On this point, see Hannes Lacher, *Beyond Globalization: Capitalism, Territoriality and the International Relations of Modernity* (New York: Routledge, 2006), 39.

27. Leo Panitch and Sam Gindin, "Superintending Global

Capital," *New Left Review* II/35 (September-October 2005): 102. For background, see also Gregory Albo and Jane Jenson, "A Contested Concept: The Relative Autonomy of the State," in *The New Canadian Political Economy*, ed. Wallace Clement and Glen Williams (Montreal: McGill-Queen's University Press, 1989), 180-211; and Leo Panitch, "The Impoverishment of State Theory," in *Paradigm Lost: State Theory Reconsidered*, ed. Stanley Aronowitz and Peter Bratsis (Minneapolis: University of Minnesota Press, 2002), 89-104.

28. Lacher, *Beyond Globalization*, 38-43.

29. For a broader critique of how an emphasis on structural reproduction hobbles Marxist economics and critical theory, see Samuel Knafo, "The Fetishizing Subject in Marx's *Capital*," *Capital and Class* 76 (2002): 145-175; and Knafo, "Critical Approaches and the Problem of Social Construction: Reassessing the Legacy of the Agent/Structure Debate in IR," Centre for Global Political Economy *Working Paper*, No. 3 (June 2008).

30. E.P. Thompson, "The Poverty of Theory or an Orrery of Errors" in E.P. Thompson, *The Poverty of Theory and other Essays* (New York: Monthly Review, 1978), 98.

31. Marx and Engels in the *Communist Manifesto*, quoted in Arrighi, *Adam Smith in Beijing*, 77.

32. Teschke, *The Myth of 1648*, 265.

33. *Ibid.* On Chinese socialism as a distinctly non-capitalist path to modernization, see Lin Chin, *The Transformation of Chinese Socialism*, especially chapter 1; and Loretta Napoleoni, *Maonomics* (New York: Seven Stories Press, 2011), chapters 1 to 5.

Chapter Four

1. Trotsky's original conception of uneven and combined development is articulated in *The Permanent Revolution and Results and Prospects* (New York: Pathfinder, 1969), and is

extended and critiqued in a recent collections of secondary articles edited by Bill Dunn and Hugo Radice, *100 Years of Permanent Revolution* (London: Pluto Press, 2006). Other important contributions include Michael Lowy, *The Politics of Combined and Uneven Development: The Theory of Permanent Revolution* (London: Verso, 1981), and the many stimulating essays collected in Alexander Anievas (ed.), *Marxism and World Politics* (New York: Routledge, 2010). My own understanding of the theory owes much to Teschke, *The Myth of 1648*, and Benno Teschke and Hannes Lacher, "The Changing 'Logics' of Capitalist Competition," *Cambridge Review of International Affairs* 20:4 (December 2007): 565-580.

2. On this point, see Ellen Wood, "Horizontal Relations: A Note on Brenner's Heresy," *Historical Materialism* 4 (Summer 1999): 178; and David McNally, *Against the Market: Political Economy, Market Socialism and the Marxist Critique* (London: Verso, 1993), 180-181.

3. Wood, "Horizontal Relations," 178.

4. McNally, *Against the Market*, 170, 185.

5. Karl Marx, "Marginal Notes to the Programme of the German Workers Party," in Karl Marx and Friedrich Engels, *Selected Works*, Volume Three (Moscow: Progress Publishers, 1970), 19.

6. These broad points and quotation from Marx are provided in McNally, 191.

7. Robin Blackburn, "Fin de Siecle: Socialism after the Crash," in Robin Blackburn (ed.), 176.

8. A useful outline of the evolving debates within the Second International on this question is provided in Norman Geras, "Rosa Luxemburg after 1905," *New Left Review* I/89 (January-February 1975): 3-46.

9. Trotsky's most powerful exposition of this argument is to be found in his *The Revolution Betrayed: What is the Soviet Union and Where is it Going?* (New York: Pathfinder Press, 1972); for

secondary elaboration and critique, see Baruch Knei-Paz, *The Social and Political Thought of Leon Trotsky* (Oxford: Clarendon Press, 1978), chapter nine; and Perry Anderson, "Trotsky's Interpretation of Stalinism," *New Left Review* I/139 (May-June 1983): 49-58.

10. On this point, see McNally, 201.

11. Mandel, "In Defence of Socialist Planning," *New Left Review* I/159 (September-October 1986), 27.

12. McNally, *Against the Market*, 193-206.

13. In addition to the works of Mandel and McNally cited above, see also Leon Trotsky, "The Soviet Economy in Danger" in Leon Trotsky, *Writings of Leon Trotsky [1932]* (New York: Pathfinder Press, 1973), 275; and Trotsky, *The Revolution Betrayed*, 67-8.

14. On this point, see McNally, 175-184.

15. See Gregor Benton, "Chinese Communism and Democracy," *New Left Review* I/148 (November-December 1984), 57-73; and Benton, *China's Urban Revolutionaries: Explorations in the History of Chinese Trotskyism, 1921-1952* (New Jersey: Humanities Press, 1996).

16. Arrighi, *Adam Smith in Beijing*, 374.

17. Maurice Meisner, *The Deng Xiaoping Era: An Inquiry into the Fate of Chinese Socialism, 1978-1994* (New York: Hill and Wang, 1996), 10; and Meisner, *Mao's China and After: A History of the People's Republic* (Revised Edition) (New York: Free Press, 1986), 46.

18. Lucien Bianco, *Origins of the Chinese Revolution, 1915-1949* (Stanford: Stanford University Press, 1971), 65.

19. There remains no better exposition of these policies than Harold R. Isaacs, *The Tragedy of the Chinese Revolution* (Chicago: Haymarket, 2010 [1938]). The recent reissuing of its original edition is of great importance for China watchers on the Left. For events in the countryside, see especially chapter 13.

20. See Knei-Paz, 358-366.

21. Benton, "Chinese Communism and Democracy," 61-62.

22. See Bianco, chapter 7.

23. Mao Tse-Tung, "On the People's Democratic Dictatorship," 30 June 1949, in Mao Tse-Tung, *Selected Works of Mao Tse-Tung*, Volume Four (Third Edition) (Beijing: Foreign Languages Press, 1969), 421.

24. Benton, "Chinese Communism and Democracy," 64.

25. *Ibid.*

26. Meisner, *Mao's China*, 70.

27. Meisner, *The Deng Xiaoping Era*, 28-29.

28. *Ibid.*, 28.

29. Maurice Meisner, *Mao's China*, 94.

30. *Ibid.*, 144-147.

31. On the continuity between the Deng regime's assessment and long-standing CCP ideology, see Claudia Pozzana and Alessandro Russo, "China's New Order and Disorders: A Dialogue Starting from Wang Hui," *Critical Asian Studies* 38:3 (2006), 349-350. On Chinese liberals portraying themselves as "true Marxists," see Arif Dirlik, "China's Critical Intelligentsia," *New Left Review* II/28 (July-August 2004):134. For arguments that Deng brought CCP ideology closer to classical Marxism, see Josef Gregory Mahoney and Xiuling Li, "A Marxist Perspective on Chinese Reforms: Interview with Jiexiong Yi," *State and Society* 73:2 (April 2009): 182-183; and Napoleoni, chapter 4.

32. Meisner, *The Deng Xiaoping Era*, 30.

33. Andreas, "Changing Colours in China," 126.

34. Ho-fung Hung, "Rise of China and the Global Overaccumulation Crisis," *Review of International Political Economy* 15:2 (2008), 154.

35. *Ibid,*, 127.

36. See, for example, the claim of Tom Bethell, for whom "property rights" constitutes history's "noblest triumph":

"Clearly, a militantly enforced Communism was sufficient to prevent most economic activity from taking place in China for 30 years..." *The Noblest Triumph*, 339.

37. Meisner, *The Deng Xiaoping Era*, 189.

38. *Ibid.*, 191.

39. *Ibid.*, 193-194.

40. *Ibid.*, 201.

41. *Ibid.*, 195.

42. *Ibid.*, 198.

43. *Ibid.*, 199.

44. On this crucial distinction, see Richard Smith, "The Chinese Road to Capitalism," *New Left Review* I/199 (May-June 1993): 56-57.

45. Hart-Landsberg and Burkett, *China and Socialism*, 8.

46. *Ibid.*, 28; Hart-Landsberg, "China, Capitalist Accumulation and the World Crisis."

47. Hart-Landsberg and Burkett, *China and Socialism*, 30.

48. *Ibid.*, 113. Hart-Landsberg also praises Maoist policies of self-reliance in "China, Capitalist Accumulation and the World Crisis," 286.

49. Anderson, "Two Revolutions," 76.

50. On decentralization during the Maoist era, see Meisner, *The Deng Xiaoping Era*, 44-45; for the Deng period, see Richard Smith, "The Chinese Road to Capitalism," 65-66; for the contemporary period, see Ho-fung Hung, "Rise of China," 159.

51. Mike Haynes, *Russia: Class and Politics, 1917-2000* (London: Bookmarks, 2002); Stephen A. Resnick and Richard Wolff, *Class Theory and History: Capitalism and Communism in the USSR* (New York: Routledge, 2002); Neil Fernandez, *Capitalism and Class Struggle in the USSR: A Marxist Theory* (Aldershot: Ashgate, 1997); Paresh Chattopadhyay, *The Marxist Concept of Capital and the Soviet Experience* (Westport: Praeger, 1994).

52. Alex Callinicos, *Imperialism and Global Political Economy* (Cambridge, UK: Polity, 2009), 275 fn.50.

53. *Ibid.*, 210.

54. Alex Callinicos, *Bonfire of Illusions: The Twin Crises of Our World* (Cambridge, UK: Polity, 2010), 118. For a similar analysis, see Neil Davidson, "China: Unevenness, Combination, Revolution?" in Dunn and Radice (eds.), 211-229. The thesis was originally applied to Russia by Tony Cliff in *State Capitalism in Russia* (London: Pluto, 1974 [1955]).

55. Mark Thomas, "Three Traditions? Marxism and the USSR," *Historical Materialism* 14.3 (2006): 207-243.

56. The past tense is being used here, but in the post-Soviet period there still remain societies that broadly fit the type, e.g. North Korea and Cuba. As noted in fn. 14, the status of post-Soviet Russia remains a disputed question.

57. Ernest Mandel was perhaps the foremost advocate of the degenerated/deformed workers' state position. See his *Power and Money: A Marxist Theory of Bureaucracy* (London: Verso, 1992). For a definitive genealogy of all three traditions, consult Marcel van der Linden, *Western Marxism and the Soviet Union* (Chicago: Haymarket Books, 2007). See also Paul Bellis, *Marxism and the U.S.S.R.: The Theory of Proletarian Dictatorship and the Marxist Analysis of Soviet Society* (New Jersey: Humanities Press, 1979).

58. Leon Trotsky, "The Class Nature of the Soviet State," 1 October 1933, in Leon Trotsky, *Writings of Leon Trotsky [1933-34]*, 112, 114.

59. Meisner, *The Deng Xiaoping Era*, 57-58.

60. Leon Trotsky, *The Transitional Program: The Death Agony of Capitalism and the Tasks of the Fourth International* (London: Bolshevik Publications, 1998), 62-63.

61. See Lacher, *Beyond Globalization*, 37; Teschke, *Myth of 1648*, 173-177.

62. Trotsky, *Revolution Betrayed*, 249.

63. Brenner's analysis was developed in articles written for *Workers' Liberty* and *Against the Current* in the late 1980s and early 1990s. The essentials of the argument are detailed in van der Linden, 284-286.
64. *Ibid.*, 284.
65. *Ibid.*, 285.
66. See the discussion of market reforms in Stalinist countries offered in Murray Smith, *Invisible Leviathan: The Marxist Critique of Market Despotism beyond Postmodernism* (Toronto: University of Toronto Press), 216.
67. In lieu of access to Brenner's original articles, I have relied upon the rendition provided by van der Linden.
68. Van der Linden, 284.
69. Teschke, *Myth of 1648*, 180.
70. *Ibid.*
71. On the importance of this even in the present, see Lin Chun, *The Transformation of Chinese Socialism*, 1-16; Napoleoni, chapters 4 and 5; and Gilley and Holbig.
72. Perry Anderson, "Two Revolutions," 79.
73. Richard Smith, "The Chinese Road," 56.
74. Perry Anderson, "Two Revolutions," 89.
75. On the bureaucracy's rationale, see Richard Smith, "The Chinese Road," 58.

Chapter Five

1. Meisner, *Mao's China and After*, 467.
2. Richard Smith, "The Chinese Road," 55-58.
3. See Jonathan Anderson, "Beijing's Exceptionalism," *The National Interest*, 100 (March-April 2009): 20.
4. Murray E.G. Smith, *Global Capitalism in Crisis: Karl Marx and the Decay of the Profit System* (Halifax: Fernwood, 2010), 29 fn. 12; Xinhua, "China's GDP growth eases to 7.8 percent in 2012," *China Daily*, 18 January 2013.
5. Richard McGregor, *The Party: The Secret World of China's*

Communist Rulers (New York: HarperCollins, 2010), 55.

6. Bethell, *The Noblest Triumph*, 341.

7. *Ibid.*, 339.

8. Hart-Landsberg and Burkett, *China and Socialism*, 31, 109.

9. My understanding of this period is informed especially by Richard Smith's "The Chinese Road to Capitalism." Unfortunately, Smith does not seem to have written an extensive update of this analysis. One subsequent article deals mainly with the environmental consequences of market reform (Richard Smith, "Creative Destruction: Capitalist Development and China's Environment," *New Left Review* I/222 (March-April 1997): 3-41); while another, co-written, article is more superficial (Nancy Holmstrom and Richard Smith, "The Necessity of Gangster Capitalism: Primitive Accumulation in Russia and China," *Monthly Review* 51:9, February 2000).

10. McGregor, *The Party*, 200.

11. Yasheng Huang, *Capitalism with Chinese Characteristics: Entrepreneurship and the State* (Cambridge: Cambridge University Press, 2008), 9.

12. McGregor, *The Party*, 200; Huang, *Capitalism with Chinese Characteristics*, 10.

13. Hart-Landsberg and Burkett, *China and Socialism*, 34.

14. *Ibid.*, 35.

15. Minqi Li, *The Rise of China*, 60.

16. Barry Naughton, "China's Distinct System: Can It be a Model for Others?" *Journal of Contemporary China* 19:65 (2010): 458.

17. Alvin So, "Peasant Conflict and the Local Predatory State in the Chinese Countryside," *Journal of Peasant Studies* 34:3 (2007), 571.

18. An especially valuable discussion of this system is to be found in Chris Bramall, "Chinese Land Reform in Long-Run Perspective and in the Wider East Asian Context," *Journal of Agrarian Change* 4:1-2 (2004): 127-130. See also Bryan Lohmar,

"Feeling for Stones But Not Crossing the River," *The Chinese Economy* 39:4 (2006): 85-102.

19. Lohmar, "Feeling for Stones But Not Crossing the River," 97.

20. On the distinction between privatization and capitalization, see Charles Post, "Comment: Primitive Accumulation in Modern China," *Dialectical Anthropology* 32 (2008): 322. On the land market in urban China, see Walker and Buck.

21. Bramall, "Chinese Land Reform in Long-Run Perspective and in the Wider East Asian Context," 130.

22. See Post, "Comment: Primitive Accumulation in Modern China"; *Dialectical Anthropology* 32 (2008): 307.

23. Richard Smith, "The Chinese Road," 64.

24. Philip C. C. Huang, *The Peasant Family and Rural Development in the Yangzi Delta, 1350-1988* (Stanford: Stanford University Press, 1990), 17-18.

25. See Philip C. C. Huang, "Beyond the Right-Left Divide: Searching for Reform from the History of Practice," *Modern China* 36:1 (2010): 115-132.

26. Bramall, "Chinese Land Reform in Long-Run Perspective and in the Wider East Asian Context," 130.

27. On technological investment and intensive labor input on Chinese farms, see Qian Forrest Zhang and John Donaldson, "The Rise of Agrarian Capitalism with Chinese Characteristics: Agricultural Modernization, Agribusiness and Collective Rights," *The China Journal* 60 (July 2008): 45.

28. *Ibid.*, 46.

29. Andreas, "Changing Colours in China," 128. See also Prem Shankar Jha, *Crouching Dragon, Hidden Tiger: Can China and India Dominate the West?* (New York: Soft Skull Press, 2010), 63-71.

30. Zhang and Donaldson, "The Rise of Agrarian Capitalism with Chinese Characteristics", 46.

31. Lynette Ong, "The Political Economy of Township Government Debt, Township Enterprises and Rural

Financial Institutions of China," *The China Quarterly* 186 (June 2006): 379; So, "Peasant conflict," 565.

32. Arrighi, *Adam Smith in Beijing*, 363; Lippit, "The Political Economy of China's Economic Reform," 449; Richard Smith, "The Chinese Road," 88-89.

33. On these dynamics, see Ong.

34. On tightening loan provisions, see Ong, "The Political Economy of Township Government Debt, Township Enterprises and Rural Financial Institutions of China," 391.

35. *Ibid.*, Ong, 391.

36. Barry Naughton, *The Chinese Economy: Transitions and Growth* (Cambridge, MA: The MIT Press, 2007), 286; Walker, 69.

37. So, "Peasant conflict," 566.

38. On the "private" form of local state corporatism, see Maria Edin, "Local state corporatism and private business," *Journal of Peasant Studies* 30:3 (2003): 279-295.

39. On structural power of the capitalist class even in the "developmental state" of South Korea, see Vivek Chibber, "The Politics of a Miracle: Class and State Power in Korean Developmentalism," in *Varieties of Capitalism, Varieties of Approaches*, ed. David Coates (New York: Palgrave Macmillan, 2005): 122-138.

40. So, "Peasant conflict," 567-568.

41. Yang Lian, "Dark Side of the Chinese Moon," *New Left Review* II/32 (March-April 2005): 135.

42. So, "Peasant conflict," 571.

43. Richard Smith, "The Chinese Road," 57-58.

44. *Ibid.*, 59.

45. *Ibid.*, 60.

46. *Ibid.*, 79-80.

47. Dic Lo, "Making Sense of China's Economic Transformation," Department of Economics Working Papers (SOAS), No. 148 (March 2006), 17; see also Dic Lo and Yu Zhang, "Globalisation Meets Its Match: Lessons from China's

Economic Transformation," *Economic and Political Weekly*, 27 December 2008.

48. Barry Naughton, *The Chinese Economy: Transitions and Growth* (Cambridge, MA: The MIT Press, 2007), 99

49. Richard Smith, "The Chinese Road," 66.

50. Richard Smith, "The Chinese Road," 70.

51. Hart-Landsberg and Burkett, *China and Socialism*, 41.

52. For the intra-party debated of the period, see McGregor, *The Party*, chapter 2.

53. Minqi Li, *The Rise of China*, 64.

54. Hart-Landsberg and Burkett, *China and Socialism*, 42.

55. See Alvin Y. So, "Beyond the Logic of Capital and the Polarization Model," 487.

56. Quoted in Christopher Marsh and Nicholas Gvosdev, "China's Yugoslav Nightmare," *The National Interest* 84 (Summer 2006): 104. From the late 1980s to the present the CCP has devoted extensive resources to the investigation of the social overturns in Eastern Europe and the Soviet Union. See David Shambaugh, *China's Communist Party: Atrophy and Adaptation* (Washington: Woodrow Wilson Center Press, 2008), chapter 4.

57. McGregor, *The Party*, 37.

Chapter Six

1. Andreas, "Changing Colours in China," 131.

2. Naughton, *The Chinese Economy*, 105.

3. *Ibid.*, 304.

4. *Ibid.*, 304.

5. *Ibid.*, 304.

6. For the bureaucracy's "neoliberal economic argument," see Hart-Landsberg and Burkett, *China and Socialism*, 43.

7. Naughton, *The Chinese Economy*, 301.

8. Javed Hamid and Stoyan Tenev, "Transforming China's Banks: the IFC's Experience," *Journal of Contemporary China*

17:56 (August 2008): 450.

9. He Li, "Debating China's Economic Reform: New Leftists vs. Liberals," *Journal of Chinese Political Science* 15 (2010): 9.

10. Hart-Landsberg and Burkett, *China and Socialism*, 43-45.

11. So, "Beyond the logic," 486.

12. Naughton, *The Chinese Economy*, 106-107.

13. Andreas, "Changing Colours in China," 132-133.

14. *Ibid.*, 140.

15. *Ibid.*

16. *Ibid.*, 133.

17. *Ibid.*, 140-141.

18. See Arrighi, "In Retrospect,"; Tom Reifer, "For Giovanni Arrighi," *New Left Review* II/60 (November-December 2009): 124; and Arrighi's articles on Africa, collected in Arrighi and Saul (eds.).

19. For an excellent analysis of the relationship between American trade unions and the Chinese working class, see Stephanie Luce and Edna Bonacich, "China and the U.S. Labor Movement" in *China and the Transformation of Global Capitalism*, ed. Ho-fung Hung (Baltimore: John Hopkins University Press, 2009): 153-173.

20. Hart-Landsberg, "The U.S. Economy and China," 15, 16.

21. *Ibid.*, 29.

22. *Ibid.*, 27.

23. Cf. Suisheng Zhao, "The China Model: Can it Replace the Western Model of Modernization?", *Journal of Contemporary China* 19:65 (2010): 419-436.

24. Mark Leonard, *What Does China Think?* (New York: PublicAffairs, 2008), 44; also, Lin Chun, "Against Privatization in China: A Historical and Empirical Account," *Journal of Chinese Political Science* 13:1 (2008): 4.

25. McGregor, *The Party*, 199.

26. *Ibid.*

27. *Ibid.* See also Sujian Guo, "The Ownership Reform in China,"

558.

28. Naughton, "The Chinese Economy," 302.

29. Shiyong Zhao, "Government Policies and Private Enterprise Development in China: 2003-2006," *China and World Economy* 17:4 (2009): 37; Naughton, "China's Distinctive System," 442.

30. Naughton, "China's Distinctive System," 444.

31. On over-competition in the world market, see Robert Brenner, *The Economics of Global Turbulence* (London: Verso, 2006).

32. Naughton, *The Chinese Economy*, 302.

33. See McGregor, *The Party*, chapter 2; Sujian Guo, 563.

34. Naughton, *The Chinese Economy*, 303.

35. Hart-Landsberg, "China, Capitalist Accumulation and the World Crisis," 275.

36. Lex, "China's new leadership," *Financial Times*, 16 November 2012.

37. Although Hart-Landsberg and Burkett even question this in "China, Capital Accumulation and Labor," 21-22.

38. He Li, "Debating China's Economic Reform", 12.

39. McGregor, *The Party*, 203.

40. FT Reporters, "To the money born," *Financial Times*, 30 March 2010. Wen Jiabao's extended family was recently reported to have amassed assets worth $2.7 billion. "China's Leaders' Image Takes Another Hit," *Wall Street Journal*, 30 October 2012.

41. Richard Daniel Ewing, "Chinese Corporate Governance and Prospects for Reform," *Journal of Contemporary China* 14:43 (May 2005): 324.

42. *Ibid.*

43. Economist, "China's flagging economy: Strong as an ox?" 24 January 2009.

44. Naughton, *The Chinese Economy*, 302.

45. Leonard, *What Does China Think?*, 44; Lex, "China's New Leadership," *Financial Times*, 16 November 2012, 16.

46. On this point, see Dic Lo, "Globalisation Meets its Match," 100.

47. Economist, "The hamster-wheel: the more China spends, the more it saves," 3 October 2009; Jeremy Page, "China Party Set to Anoint Next Leaders," *Wall Street Journal*, 8 November 2012.

48. John Hassard, Jackie Sheehan and Xiao Yuxin, "Chinese State Enterprise Reform: Economic Transition, Labour Unrest and Worker Representation," *Capital and Class* 96 (2008): 38.

49. *Ibid.*, 488.

50. Naughton, *The Chinese Economy*, 304; Hart-Landsberg, "China, Capitalist Accumulation and the World Crisis," 275.

51. Naughton, *The Chinese Economy*, 303.

52. Brenner, *The Economics of Global Turbulence*, 340.

53. Ho-fung Hung, "Rise of China and the Global Overaccumulation Crisis," 159.

54. *Ibid.*

55. *Ibid.*

56. Godfrey Yeung, "How Banks in China make Lending Decisions," *Journal of Contemporary China* 18:59 (March 2009): 300.

57. Hung, "Rise of China and the Global Overaccumulation Crisis," 158.

58. *Ibid.*, 158.

59. *Ibid.*, 160.

60. Feng Chen, "Industrial Restructuring and Workers' Resistance in China," *Modern China* 29: 2 (April 2003): 239-240.

61. Quoted in *Ibid.*, 248.

62. Chen's use of the *Workers' Daily* as the basis for his investigation may bias the data. The media organ could have disproportionately reported those cases in which workers' appeals were successful in order to portray the party-state as a responsive ally of the working class.

63. *Ibid.*, 254-255.
64. Hassard, Sheehan and Yuxin, "Chinese State Enterprise Reform," 45.
65. *Ibid.*, 46-47.
66. On the latter, see He Li, and more recently Mark Leonard, "The affluence trap," *New Statesman*, 11-17 January 2013. The broad contours of contemporary intellectual and political debate in China are sketched out well in Leonard, *What Does China Think?*, especially chapter 1.
67. Economist, "The Second Long March," 13 December 2008.
68. Weil, "Conditions of the Working Classes in China," 39.
69. Ho-fung Hung partly recognizes this but does not draw out its implications for assessing Chinese capitalism. See Hung, "Rise of China and the Global Overaccumulation Crisis," 160.
70. Hassard, Sheehan and Yuxin, "Chinese State Enterprise Reform," 48.
71. Of course, they were hardly alone in this—many, if not most, critical scholars predicted the same.
72. Economist, "The next China," 31 July 2010.
73. Economist, "Reflating the dragon," 15 November 2008. For more on this program and how it defied the doomy predictions of Western economists and financial journalists, see Loretta Napoleoni, *Maonomics* (New York: Seven Stories Press, 2011), chapter 11.
74. Economist, "Decoupling 2.0," 23 May 2009.
75. Michael Wines, "China Fortifies State Businesses to Fuel Growth," *New York Times*, 29 August 2010; Jamil Anderlini, "The thin red line," *Financial Times*, 16 November 2012.
76. Economist, "Nationalisation rides again," 14 November 2009.
77. See Economist, "Reflating the dragon," 15 November 2008.
78. Economist, "The hamster-wheel," 3 October 2009.
79. On the New Right see Leonard, *What Does China Think?*,

chapter one; and Leonard, "The affluence trap."

80. Economist. "Still not the tiller." 25 October 2008.
81. Cf. Qin Hui, "Dividing the Big Family Assets," *New Left Review* II/20 (March-April 2003): 83-110.
82. So, "Peasant conflict."
83. Bill Schiller, "Saving the Family Farm," *Toronto Star*, 15 November 2008.
84. Zhang and Donaldson, "The Rise of Agrarian Capitalism with Chinese Characteristics," 44.
85. Weil, "City of Youth," 41.
86. Leonard, *What Does China Think?*, 20.
87. Economist, "A time for muscle-flexing," 21 March 2009.
88. Eva Cheng, "Resistance against capitalist restoration in China," *Links: A Journal of Socialist Renewal*, 29 (2006).
89. See Yasheng Huang, "Democratize or Die: Why China's Communists Face Reform or Revolution," *Foreign Affairs*, 92:1(January-February 2013): 47-54; Economist, "Chasing the Chinese Dream," 4 May 2013.
90. Bloomberg News, "Xi Jinping Millionaire Relations Reveal Fortunes of Elite," 29 June 2012, http://www.bloomberg.com/news/2012-06-29/xi-jinping-millionaire-relations-reveal-fortunes-of-elite.html.
91. Economist, "Chasing the Chinese Dream," 4 May 2013.
92. Abheek Bhattacharya, "China's Anti-Keynesian Insurgent," 15 October 2012.

Chapter Seven
1. Arrighi, *The Long Twentieth Century*, 396-370.
2. For Japan, see Burkett and Hart-Landsberg, "The Use and Abuse of Japan as a Progressive Model" in *Socialist Register 1996: Are There Alternatives?*, ed. Leo Panitch (London: Merlin, 1996), 62-92; for South Korea, see Hart-Landsberg, *The Rush to Development: Economic Change and Political Struggle in South Korea* (New York: Monthly Review Press,

1993).

3. Rory Carroll, "Capitalist storm clouds loom over Havana after state cuts 1M jobs," *Guardian*, 14 September 2009; John Arlidge, "Castro calls up Cuba's Bransons," *Sunday Times* [London], 5 May 2013.

4. Panitch, "Giovanni Arrighi in Beijing," 86.

Contemporary culture has eliminated both the concept of the public and the figure of the intellectual. Former public spaces – both physical and cultural – are now either derelict or colonized by advertising. A cretinous anti-intellectualism presides, cheerled by expensively educated hacks in the pay of multinational corporations who reassure their bored readers that there is no need to rouse themselves from their interpassive stupor. The informal censorship internalized and propagated by the cultural workers of late capitalism generates a banal conformity that the propaganda chiefs of Stalinism could only ever have dreamt of imposing. Zer0 Books knows that another kind of discourse – intellectual without being academic, popular without being populist – is not only possible: it is already flourishing, in the regions beyond the striplit malls of so-called mass media and the neurotically bureaucratic halls of the academy. Zer0 is committed to the idea of publishing as a making public of the intellectual. It is convinced that in the unthinking, blandly consensual culture in which we live, critical and engaged theoretical reflection is more important than ever before.